Charlotte Markey,
Daniel Hart & Douglas N. Zacher

Illustrated by @DanTheScribbler

BEING YOU

THE BODY IMAGE BOOK FOR BOYS

CAMBRIDGE
UNIVERSITY PRESS

University Printing House, Cambridge CB2 8BS, United Kingdom

One Liberty Plaza, 20th Floor, New York, NY 10006, USA

477 Williamstown Road, Port Melbourne, VIC 3207, Australia

314–321, 3rd Floor, Plot 3, Splendor Forum, Jasola District Centre, New Delhi – 110025, India

103 Penang Road, #05-06/07, Visioncrest Commercial, Singapore 238467

Cambridge University Press is part of the University of Cambridge.

It furthers the University's mission by disseminating knowledge in the pursuit of education, learning, and research at the highest international levels of excellence.

www.cambridge.org
Information on this title: www.cambridge.org/9781108949378
DOI: 10.1017/9781108954242

First published 2022

Printed in Singapore by Markono Print Media Pte Ltd

A catalogue record for this publication is available from the British Library

ISBN 978-1-108-94937-8 Paperback

For Charlie

ENDORSEMENTS

"With suicide rates surging for preteen and teenage boys – yet another painful sign of their feeling trapped by impossible pressures – and the top 15 causes of premature mortality predominantly male, how they relate to their bodies plainly matters. In their colorful, evidence-based, and wonderfully accessible book, the authors bring wisdom, compassion, and even humor to a subject that has been shrouded in myth for generations. For parents, educators, and coaches who understand that integrity begins with how well a child cares for himself, an attitude learned – or not – early in life, I heartily recommend this book."

Michael C. Reichert, PhD, *Executive Director, Center for the Study of Boys' and Girls' Lives, University of Pennsylvania*

"Parents who have been asking for ways to support their sons' body image have a new resource to share with their adolescents. *Being You* meets boys where they are and offers research, personal stories, and practical guidance for navigating the confusing messages young men receive from the culture. This book also serves as a much-needed conversation-starter for families about what it means to take care of your authentic self, inside and out."

Oona Hanson, *Educator and Parent Coach*

"Dr. Markey has done it again! *Being You: The Body Image Book for Boys* is an excellent companion book to her body image book for girls. The chapters cover critical body image issues that boys would want to know: puberty, how they can take care of their bodies, and eating. The coverage of related mental health issues like bullying and self-compassion makes for a well-rounded volume of how boys can learn to be their best selves. Body image and eating issues are increasing for boys, and need more attention from researchers, parents, and media. A book like this is necessary to help guide boys through body image issues in a way that is fun, engaging, and specific to boys' needs and concerns. It's beautifully illustrated and highly readable, and features real-life stories from boys and expert advice. Give the boys in your life a gift they deserve—buy this book!"

Dr Meghan Gillen, *Associate Professor of Psychology, Penn State Abington*

"Teen boys face immense body image pressures from social media and peers now more than ever, but these important issues are rarely acknowledged or discussed. *Being You: The Body Image Book for Boys* is an invaluable resource designed for boys to promote a positive body image based on the latest scientific evidence, expert advice, and real-life stories."

Jason Nagata, MD, *University of California, San Francisco*

"This is a terrific book. *Being You* frankly and kindly guides adolescent boys to develop a positive body image in terms of what they can't change, what they can indeed learn to do, and the wisdom and self-compassion to learn the difference. With a skillful blend of definitions and explanations, plus advice from experts and a diverse set of adolescent boys and young men, the authors deftly transform scientific research findings into practical advice that respects the desires, needs, stressors, and appearance concerns of adolescent boys. Parents, grandparents, pediatricians, teachers, clergy, and others would also do well to read this book – if only to study the sensible chapters on puberty and nutrition and to be prepared to challenge the many sociocultural messages that make it all too easy for boys to use the petri dish of toxic masculinity to cultivate a negative body image and other unhealthy habits."

Michael P. Levine, PhD, FAED, *Emeritus Professor of Psychology, Kenyon College*

"*The Body Image Book for Boys* contains every single piece of information that doctors and experts want teenage boys to know- but rarely get the chance to tell them…

Delivered with a thoughtful, empathetic, and intelligent tone, and filled with detailed, evidence-based content, this book is ideal for boys who are hungry for knowledge about what is happening in their bodies, and how best to look after their physical and mental health.

The authors communicate complex issues and information in interesting and detailed ways. They dispel the myths, and share the stories of numerous adolescent boys with a range of different attitudes toward, or experiences of, their bodies. This book covers such a wide range of topics - the physical, the emotional, and everything in between. Strongly recommend."

Dr Zali Yager, *Executive Director, The Body Confident Collective*

"The ultimate handbook to help boys navigate puberty and develop a healthy body image. Packed full of practical and evidence-based advice on diet, fitness, and mental health, it addresses boys' body image concerns head-on.

A must read. *Being You* will help boys appreciate they have more to offer the world than how they look."

Judi Craddock, Author of *The Little Book of Body Confidence*

"While reading *Being You: The Body Image Book for Boys*, I kept thinking, "finally!" Finally, we publicly recognize that boys are just as privy to societal standards for unrealistic, perfect bodies and the pressure to still try to conform. Finally, we give boys the tools to recognize these problems and find solutions for themselves and peers. This book is jam-packed with the basics boys need to know about their physical and mental health as well as the red flag behaviors and conditions to watch out for. The writing style translates research and terminology into understandable concepts, along with quotes from professionals and stories from older adolescents. As I read, I reflected on the patients I've seen in my Pediatrics and Adolescent Medicine training who would have greatly benefited from this book and am excited for the boys I get to recommend it to very soon."

Rebekah Fenton, MD, *Pediatrician and Adolescent Health Advocate, Ann & Robert H. Lurie Children's Hospital of Chicago*

"What a great resource for boys! As a society, we don't spend enough time talking to boys about positive body image and healthy development. This book provides boys and their families with powerful, evidence-based information and advice about how to take care of themselves and their bodies physically and psychologically during the teen years. It is engaging and fun and provides stories from real boys and young men as well as advice from experts. I wholeheartedly recommend it!"

Elizabeth Daniels, PhD, *Associate Professor, Director of the MA Program in Psychological Science, Director of the Undergraduate Honors Program, University of Colorado Colorado Springs*

"*Being You* dispels the myth of body image only being a concern for girls and provides an excellent, insightful analysis of the nature of body image concerns among boys, as well as what causes these concerns. It also discusses when body image concerns are likely to cause significant problems for boys and what can be done to address these concerns.

Dr Markey and her colleagues have provided a well-informed, engaging and thoughtful analysis of the above issues. The book adopts a positive approach to body, exploring how boys can engage in healthy physical activity and eating so that they experience physical and mental health.

I love the engaging layout of the book – from boy's stories to expert advice, to useful tips to address concerns that are unique to boys. The book is clearly well researched by the authors, who are experts in the field, but is also written in an accessible way for boys, their parents, teachers and others who work with boys. A wonderful book that will be a central resource to all who are interested in ensuring that boys grow up to be healthy and well-adjusted men."

Professor Marita McCabe PhD, FAPS, FCCLP, FCHP, *Research Professor and Team Leader, Health and Ageing Research Group, Swinburne University*

"A big shout out to *Being You*! This is the book we need right now to help boys navigate the increasingly difficult terrain of maturing into men. The punchy, graphical format makes it a good fit for today's adolescent attention spans. The authors wisely place body image in wider contexts, ranging from unrealistic social media images of ripped men to the perils of diet fads to the need to challenge confined definitions of masculinity itself. Boys will be better boys thanks to this book!"

Ed Frauenheim, co-author of *Reinventing Masculinity: The Liberating Power of Compassion and Connection*

"Finally, a book dedicated to the experience of boys and body image. It's not just an issue that impacts girls, in fact, anyone with a body has a sense of their own body image. Drs Markey, Hart and Zacher write about the unique experiences of boys and men and their relationship with their bodies such as feeling the pressure to be lean and muscular. The scientific research presented in each chapter is supported by the stories of real boys and men in their own voices which makes the content highly relatable. There is also a range of great tips to help boys improve their sense of body image as well as encouragement for boys to become the changemakers in promoting positive body image in society more generally. This book is a highly useful resource for boys and everyone who supports them."

Dr Gemma Sharp, *Senior Research Fellow & Clinical Psychologist, Leader, Body Image Research Unit, Department of Psychiatry, Monash University*

"This book gives boys the crucial skills and language to talk about – and hopefully improve – the relationship they have with their bodies. These conversations are often taboo for both men and boys, but this book provides the necessary roadmap to tackle them in a compassionate and productive way. In short, this book is a must for anyone trying to support the young boys and men in their lives."

Jeffrey Hunger, PhD, *Assistant Professor of Social Psychology, Department of Psychology, Miami University, Ohio*

ABOUT THE AUTHORS

Dr. Charlotte Markey is a world-leading expert in body image research, having studied all things body image, eating behavior, and weight management for her entire adult life (about 25 years!). She is passionate about understanding what makes us feel good about our bodies and helping people to develop a healthy body image. Charlotte loves to share her body image wisdom with others, and is an experienced book author, blogger, and Professor of Psychology at Rutgers University, Camden. She currently lives in Pennsylvania with her son, Charlie, her daughter, Grace, her husband, Dan, and their dog, Lexi. For fun, she likes to run, travel, and read, but often spends her free time nagging her kids to brush their teeth or remove the cups and dishes from their rooms.

To learn more about Charlotte Markey, you can visit her website at www. CharlotteMarkey.com or connect with her on Facebook (Dr. Charlotte Markey), Twitter (@char_markey), Instagram (@char_markey), or YouTube (Body Positivity).

Dr. Daniel Hart is a developmental psychologist and distinguished Professor of Psychology at Rutgers University, Camden, who has studied and worked with adolescents and young adults for more than 30 years. He has written several books, including *Becoming Men*. Dan is passionate about understanding factors that lead to healthy development, especially when young people experience disadvantaged upbringings. Dan likes to visit his daughter and her partner and his son, daughter-in-law, and granddaughters as much as possible. He enjoys teasing Charlie and Grace and hiking, reading, and playing basketball in his free time. To learn more about Daniel Hart, you can visit his website at www.hart.camden. rutgers.edu.

Douglas Zacher, MA, has a long-standing interest in issues pertaining to mental health, eating, education, and public policy. He is currently a doctoral student in the Department of Public Affairs/Community Development at Rutgers University, Camden, where he is also a part-time lecturer teaching classes including Introduction to Psychology. Doug conducted many of the interviews that appear in this book and made sure that his (somewhat) older collaborators didn't sound completely out of touch. In his free time, he enjoys working on computers, reading and watching comics, hiking and camping, and playing video games. You can connect with Doug on Twitter at @ZacherDouglas.

CONTENTS

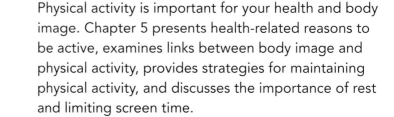

Chapter 6: Fuel your body · · · · · · · · · · 105

Because what you eat will impact your body, it's important to understand what scientists know about how to eat healthily. This chapter will help you understand the basics of nutritional science.

Chapter 7: Forget food fads · · · · · · · · · · 133

Food fads—such as removing certain food groups from your diet—are bad for our body image and are physically and psychologically unhealthy. This chapter focuses on reasons to avoid these fads and focus on habits that are good for you for the long haul.

Chapter 8: Love to eat · · · · · · · · · · 158

It's so important to enjoy food! This chapter addresses the ways a healthy diet nourishes you physically and psychologically, and can include celebrations and comfort food. It also examines eating disorders and the links between eating habits and mental health.

Chapter 9: Building the best you · · · · · · · · · · 186

This chapter provides strategies for taking care of your mental and physical health. Everyone can use extra support at one time or another.

Chapter 10: Make a difference · · · · · · · · · · 210

Developing a positive body image is so important for your own well-being and for the positive change you can contribute to the world around you.

CHAPTER ONE

WHAT IS BODY IMAGE?

#BodyImageIsForBoys

"IT TAKES COURAGE TO GROW UP AND BECOME WHO YOU REALLY ARE."

E.E. Cummings, American poet

You're probably wondering why your mom (or dad, or teacher, or aunt) bought you this book. You've heard the term "body image" before, but you've never thought of it as particularly relevant to you. In fact, maybe you aren't even sure exactly what it is. If you've ever wished that you were taller, leaner, had different hair, bigger muscles, or you were different in some other way, this book is for you.

In this chapter you'll learn

○ how body image is defined,
○ why it's important to have a positive body image, and
○ why reading this book and developing a positive body image will improve your life.

In the past, many thought that only girls had concerns about body image. No longer! The latest research suggests that boys and men are concerned about the appearances of their bodies and related issues just about as much as girls and women are. You'll learn about boys' bodies and body images in this book, and how to protect your health. Perhaps most importantly, **you'll learn about being *you*— accepting who you are and growing into the best version of yourself.** Some days, growing up may feel easy; other days, it may feel really difficult. On the next page, Thomas describes how he's learning to feel comfortable with who he is and to focus his energy on what he thinks is most important in his life.

This book addresses the issues that Thomas faced and the many questions and concerns that boys like you may have about body image. It will offer you healthy and effective ways to be happy with your body and yourself.

THOMAS DAVID, 16 YEARS OLD

Toward the end of middle school (8th grade), some kids at school started to say stuff to me about my weight. They acted like they were just joking around, but I knew better. By that time, I was a bit **overweight** and already uncomfortable about how I looked. The teasing only made me want to lose some weight and start working out more. Sometimes I go to the gym with my friends and that can be motivating. I can't say that I've fully gotten into good **exercise** habits quite yet.

I wish I felt more comfortable in my body and felt less self-conscious. I have nice eyes and I guess my face is the best part of my body. I suppose it could be worse! But I can't say I particularly like the rest of my appearance.

If I could offer advice to younger boys, I'd say two things. First, don't pick on each other. It's hard enough to feel good in your own skin; no one needs to be getting negative feedback from others. And two, don't feel **self-conscious**. I wish I wasn't so self-conscious when I was younger. Kids shouldn't be scared of what their bodies are. There are so many more important things in the world.

EXPERT ADVICE

Hayden Cedric Dawes, *counselor, USA*

"I fear, in our visually driven **society**, that boys and men increasingly struggle with body **acceptance**. We need to open up our conversations about these issues to boys and men so that they can love their bodies as they are."

WHAT IS BODY IMAGE?

Body image is how you think and feel about your body. The way you think and feel about your body—your body image—matters. For example, if you wish you had bigger biceps, you may spend a lot of time in the gym lifting weights. If you want to be thinner, you may try to remove carbs from your diet (see Chapter 6 for all the reasons this is not a good idea!). If you wish that your ears didn't stick out as much as they do, you may consider getting surgery to change them.

But what if there are better ways to address your concerns about your appearance? Maybe changing how you look to fit in or to look a certain way isn't the answer. Maybe there is an easier way. **This book is full of information and advice about body image that will help you understand your body and develop** positive **feelings about it.**

Still not convinced that this book is for you? Take the quiz on the opposite page and then read how to score it.

These questions come from surveys that researchers have used to study body image, eating behaviors, and disordered eating among boys and men. If you answered "yes" to any of these questions, this book is definitely for you. Even if you came close to answering "yes" to any of these questions, read on!

There is nothing wrong with you if you pay attention to what you eat or care about how you look. Most people do. However, some of these thoughts may be healthy and some of them may not be. This book will help you stay on the path toward health and avoid problems that many boys and men experience when it comes to their body images, self-esteem, eating behaviors, and mental and physical health. **We want you to love being *you*.**

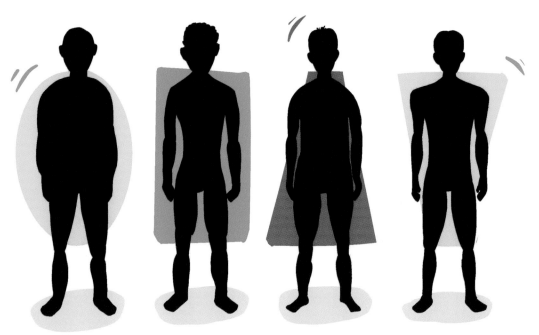

Boy's eating, weight, and body image survey	YES	NO
I worry about how I look.		
I don't always feel very good about myself.		
I am currently trying to change my weight.		
I am trying to gain weight or build muscle.		
What I eat has influenced how I think about myself as a person.		
If I break any of my food rules, I attempt to make up for it at my next meal.		
I don't feel like other people accept me as I am.		
I have continued eating despite feeling full, in an attempt to influence my muscularity.		
I have used meal-replacement supplements.		
I have added protein-based supplements to my diet.		
Other people do not seem to understand my food choices.		
I wish I could have more respect for myself.		
There are definitely foods I have avoided eating due to worry about how they might affect my shape or weight.		

We also want to increase thoughtful conversations about boys' and men's health. Unfortunately, boys and men tend to talk about health issues less often than girls and women do. It has sometimes been viewed as more macho or manly for boys and men not to talk about their (emotional) feelings or how they feel physically. Communication about health issues is critically important in order for all people—regardless of their gender identification—to feel good! We want this book to help answer all sorts of questions that you may have about your health, and also to increase your awareness of issues that may affect other people you know. By being educated about the issues we discuss in this book, you will be in a position to improve not only your own health, but others' health as well.

EXPERT ADVICE

Oona Hanson, *educator and health advocate, USA*

"When it comes to body image, many boys feel competing pressures—not wanting to be 'too small' while also being afraid of being 'too fat.' Because our culture links appearance concerns with girls, many boys wonder if something is wrong with them simply for caring about how they look. It's normal to feel **self-conscious** at times and to be aware of how others perceive you. But be careful about comparing your unique self to images you see—not only celebrities, athletes, and others in the media, but also your peers. And here's a secret: even those people who seem 'perfect' on the outside often struggle with anxiety about their looks. Shifting your focus to respecting and caring for your own body will improve your **well-being** and leave you with more energy for the things that matter most."

In each chapter of this book, be on the lookout for different features. We've designed this book so you don't have to read it from cover to cover for it to make sense. You can skip around (the index in the back of the book will tell you where to find certain topics) and read the features that you enjoy the most and find the most helpful.

In each chapter, you'll find:

- **Reliable information:** We summarize the latest science on the topic. If you see a word you don't know, check the glossary in the back of this book.

As you read, remember you're a member of a large community that cares about these issues. We don't know many people who haven't given these issues some thought or had concerns about them.

- **Q & A:** During our careers, we've talked with hundreds of boys. For this book, we've asked them what questions they have about their bodies, eating, exercising, and all the other topics in this book. We provide factual answers to their questions—which are probably the ones you have, too. Below is an example.

Most of my friends are a lot taller than me. I hope that I catch up at some point. How do I know when I am done growing taller?

Many boys will notice that they grow fastest during middle school (10–14 years, approximately) as they enter puberty and experience a growth spurt. However, boys often continue to get taller throughout high school (14–18 years, approximately) and even after high school. It is possible that you will keep growing until you are 20 years old. As we'll discuss in Chapter 3, boys' experiences of puberty, which includes a growth spurt, vary a lot. The timing of the growth spurt varies from person to person; you may have friends who grow a lot in 6th grade, and others who get taller most quickly in 10th grade. One final thought: differences in height between people are largely determined by our genes. In other words, the majority of differences in height are due to our biology. Height is like shoe size—it's not something you can change. And what is the "perfect height" anyway?

- **Myths and misbeliefs:** In each chapter, we share "myths and misbeliefs" about body image and related topics and explain why they aren't true. Here is an example:

MYTHS & MISBELIEFS

> Boys don't—or shouldn't—cry. Being emotionally sensitive is a sign of weakness.

Boys often feel they're getting the message that it's really important to look strong (for example, muscular) and also that they are strong (for example, not emotional or sensitive). However, it is perfectly normal to have strong emotions; expressing your feelings is completely normal and healthy. In fact, some scientific research suggests that people who believe they must inhibit their emotions are vulnerable to health problems. Writing and talking about emotional experiences may improve how you feel physically and psychologically, and may even help to improve your immune functioning (your ability to fight off infections and maintain health).

Being "masculine" does not mean that you can't be sensitive. If another boy or man ever teases you for being emotional it is most likely because *he* feels uncomfortable. Resist suggestions from others that you shouldn't express sadness and other strong emotions.

- **My story:** In the process of writing this book, we've relied on scientific research that takes into account hundreds and thousands of boys' experiences. But we've also interviewed individual boys, like Thomas David (his story is earlier in this chapter) and Mateo Carlos (his story is at the end of this chapter). These boys are all in their teens and twenties, and they shared their specific experiences in detail. Each chapter highlights some of these real boys' experiences, in their own voices.

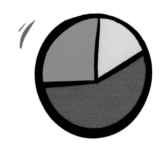

- **Inspiration:** When it comes to feeling good about our bodies, we can all use some inspiration. Each chapter contains quotes, illustrations, and bits of information to help you think about your body and yourself in a positive way—and maybe even laugh about some of the issues that you've found stressful.

- **Ask the expert:** In the process of writing this book, we haven't only talked to hundreds of boys like you, we've also talked with experts. Sometimes what they've said is so helpful that we quote their advice. Look for these quotes throughout the chapters. Here's a quote from one of the first scientists to study body image among boys:

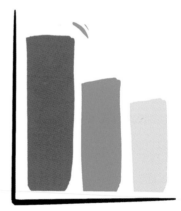

EXPERT ADVICE

Professor Marita McCabe, PhD,
Swinburn University, Australia

"When I started my research on male body image concerns in the 1990s, it was generally accepted that boys were not worried about the size and shape of their bodies—this was a girl problem. However, in our research we found that we were asking boys the wrong questions—we were asking questions that were relevant for girls, not boys, things like wanting to be slim or lose weight. Our research, and that of many other researchers, has now shown that even young boys are concerned about their bodies, but they are often focused on having a lean, strong, muscular body, rather than being thin."

- **Find out more:** The information in this book is **evidence-based** and scientific in nature. In other words, the ideas in this book are not based on our opinions, but on the work of thousands of scientists. If you want to read more about a topic, we provide references to this scientific work, which is a good place to start.

We provide you with the latest information so that you can grow up to be passionate, caring, and physically and emotionally healthy. Once you know the facts about the smartest way to develop a positive body image, you will have the tools that will help you to become your best self.

MY STORY

MATEO CARLOS, 20 YEARS OLD

When I was younger, I used to hate my body. I was heavy and I couldn't enjoy myself and I was really out of shape. I would find myself out of breath within 10 seconds of doing any **physical activity**. I also didn't like what I saw when I looked at myself in the mirror. Currently, I am still somewhat heavy, but I am pleased with my body. I don't deprive myself of foods that I enjoy, but I try to not eat too many sweet treats.

The thing that has changed is that I work out, exercise, and play sports as much as I can. I do this because I enjoy it and I know it is good for me. I've also been able to notice myself feeling stronger and I get to spend time with my family and friends while being physically active. I've been able to meet so many people because of sports and I never regret the time I spend playing sports. When I was in middle school, I couldn't run a single mile without completely dying, but by the time I was in high school, I was running 3.5 miles and still feeling good afterwards.

My friends and family have been influential in terms of how I think about my body. I was often bullied about my weight, and my friends and family helped me have a stronger sense of myself. I've come to appreciate that everybody has a different body type. Although some things might work for your friends or family, that doesn't mean it's going to work for you too. And that's okay. Don't beat yourself up over it. Don't let anybody tell you who you are—that's up to you to decide.

Summing Up #BodyImageIsForBoys

- ☑ Body image is defined as how you think and feel about your body.
- ☑ Your body image may affect your physical health, mental and emotional well-being, and your health behaviors.
- ☑ Understanding your body image and knowing how to develop a positive body image will benefit you across your entire life.

Find out more

- Dr. Stuart Murray and Dr. Jason Negata are two of the leading scientists studying body image and eating concerns among boys and men. The questionnaire in this chapter is adapted from some of their research.

- For more scholarly articles and web pages with information about body image, see the companion website to this book: www. theBodyImageBookforBoys.com

CHAPTER TWO

BECOME BODY CONFIDENT

#LoveYourselfFirst

> "A MAN CANNOT BE COMFORTABLE WITHOUT HIS OWN APPROVAL."
>
> Mark Twain, American writer

Does anyone truly feel good about their body?

If you look on Instagram or YouTube, it seems like everyone is trying to change their bodies. Most people aren't all that satisfied with what they see when they look in the mirror, at least not after they hit **adolescence**.

Can you *learn* to feel good about your body?

We don't think much about our bodies when we're young children, but as adolescence approaches, we become critical of them. We wish our biceps were bigger or our noses were smaller. We wish for clearer skin and more **muscular** abs. But why? A six-pack, big biceps, and clear skin don't make us smarter or nicer people. The desire for these physical features is learned. What has been learned can be *unlearned*.

In this chapter you'll learn

- ○ some tips to help you stay positive about your body,
- ○ the importance of nurturing a positive body image and keeping others from being negative influences on your body image, and
- ○ the difference between **adaptive appearance investment** and caring too much about your appearance.

There is good **scientific evidence** that you can improve how you feel about your body. You can even feel great about how you look (at least most of the time!). It's not about changing your body so that you look more like Ronaldo, one of the most famous soccer players of all time, or Tom Holland, the latest Spiderman, and Chris Evans, Captain America himself. It's more about changing how you think about yourself. There are influences all around you—action figures, real-life athletes, movie stars, and **influencers**—that you may feel you don't measure up to. It is important to realize that there will always be someone who is taller, more muscular, more **athletic**, or better looking than you. Don't let your looks determine your value and worth. Love yourself first for who you are as a person.

EXPERT ADVICE

Professor Tracy Tylka, PhD, *Ohio State University, USA*

"Having a positive body image means that you appreciate your body, which helps you **respect** and care for it. You don't focus on how your body looks as much as how it feels and all the cool things it is able to do. It's so important to build a positive body image because it can help you feel good about yourself and cope with **stress** in healthy ways. Overall, a positive body image can offer peace of mind."

FOCUS ON FUNCTIONALITY

What is **functionality**? Functionality refers to the ways in which your body moves, works, or functions. Our bodies perform all sorts of functions each and every day. We walk, run, jump, eat, sleep, breathe, sing, swim, climb, and a million other actions. Our bodies make all of these things possible.

Scientists who study body image have found that thinking about our bodies' functionality is important. In fact, the more we think about functionality, the less we seem to get hung up on more **superficial** issues of appearance. If you're ever feeling discouraged about your body, it can be helpful to spend a bit of time thinking about the things your body does. Start with what you did when you woke up this morning and think about everything you did during your day. Maybe you woke up, showered, got dressed and ready for school, ate breakfast, rode your bike to school, read, wrote, completed a

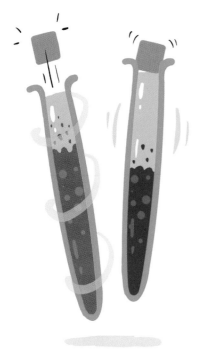

science experiment, talked to your friends, ate lunch, ran during gym class, played soccer, finished your homework, ate dinner, spent time with your family, watched television, and got ready for bed. Your body made all of that possible. That's a lot!

Your body digested your food and used that for **energy** to ride your bike and stay alert at school. Your brain allowed you to do your schoolwork and to have conversations with your friends and family. Coordination between your body and your brain allowed you to play baseball. Your body is truly amazing.

How do you help your body complete so many amazing tasks? You feed it, you keep it clean by bathing and following other good **hygiene** practices, and you sleep. When you think about it, you don't have to do all that much to end up with a body that can do so many things. As Jai came to understand, he feels better when he spends some time taking care of himself by exercising and avoiding a lot of **fast food**.

JAI PARTH, 21 YEARS OLD

Overall, I feel positively about my body. I like my height and I'm glad that I'm a bit taller than average. I do sometimes think that I should be going to the gym more often. My father and grandfather have big bellies that they are trying to get rid of. I don't want to end up with a big belly when I get older, but I also don't want to just be obsessed with exercising.

I am an international student and when I first came to America, the fast-food culture and food options on campus excited me and I gained a lot of weight. When I moved from India, my cousin was the first person I met and spent a lot of time with. He is a "gymaholic." I went to the gym with him. My cousin has a flat stomach and good abs that I'm somewhat envious of. Later, when I joined a fraternity, many of the guys I met would work out on a regular basis and so I started to go more often as well. If I have someone to go with to the gym, I will go and I like how it makes me feel.

Body image in India is not a big concern. If you are overweight, it is not a concern. When I came to America, it became obvious that many people have health problems that may be related to being overweight. I do believe that if you don't take care of your body, later down the road you will be more prone to disease. Many people have diseases like type 2 **diabetes** because they haven't taken care of their body.

My advice for younger boys is to think about their bodies as a series of choices. You can choose to exercise. You can choose to eat well. You can choose to take care of yourself. At the end of the day, these are choices that everyone makes. I cut down a lot on eating fast food because I realized it wasn't making me feel good. But if you feel good and you are confident, then you don't have to change anything about yourself. The way other people think about your body should not influence the way you think about it.

APPRECIATE YOUR BODY

Even though your body is amazing, you may be able to come up with things you don't like about it. What things lead you to think negatively about your body? Can you avoid them? For example, if looking at Instagram influencers' abs leads you to feel bad about yourself, you could avoid Instagram or, at the very least, unfollow people who make you feel bad and replace them with body-positive accounts like @zachmiko, @thechrismosier, or @realryansheldon. (There are more body-positive social media accounts across different platforms listed in Chapter 10.)

Even though guys don't always talk about these issues, you aren't alone if you don't always feel great about your body. It seems that guys can act like their concerns about their body are "no big deal," while at the same time they'll complain to body image psychologists about the unfair and impossible standards regarding what men are supposed to look like. Guys will also admit to strict meal plans, intense exercise, feeling depressed, and avoiding social situations because they don't feel confident about their bodies or their looks in general.

Just because it is "normal" for guys to feel dissatisfied with their bodies doesn't mean that this is healthy. There are a lot of things you can do to feel better and be your best self. One activity that may help you feel better about your body is to make a mental list of the things that you like (or love) about your body and appearance. These can be anything: your eyes, teeth, hair, fingernails, feet, stomach, calves, arms—anything at all. Think about why you love these parts of yourself. Maybe your teeth are nice and straight after years of wearing braces. Maybe you like that your feet are big or your eyes are blue. Maybe you like the haircut you currently have, or your long arms that help you play basketball. You don't need to write this down or share this with anyone, so you can brag to yourself all you want. When you feel down on yourself or upset about some aspect of your appearance, think about your list of the qualities you like about your body. Take a moment to feel grateful for them and focus on them rather than on negative thoughts about your appearance.

Scientists who study body image refer to an appreciation of, gratitude for, and caring about one's body as a positive body image. Although many people find fault with parts of their bodies or their appearance, they may not feel crippling dissatisfaction. Aim higher than *not feeling bad* about your body, but to actually *feeling good* about it. It's like aiming to be happy instead of *not* being depressed. Focusing on appreciating your body and being grateful for aspects of your appearance *can improve how you feel* about your body and appearance. In one of the studies we conducted with some other researchers, we asked people to list only *three* features they were grateful for about their appearance. Even just making this very short list had a positive impact on people's body image. It's a simple thing to do, but it works!

EXPERT ADVICE

Zoë Bisbing and **Leslie Bloch**, counselors and body image educators, USA

"Boys and men are often left out of conversations about body image, but they experience cultural pressure around their own appearance ideals. Their idealized body looks different from the ideal for girls and women—it involves bulking up muscles, gaining weight, and losing body fat—but it's also getting progressively more unattainable over time. At the same time, we aren't preparing our boys with the language and tools to cope with that pressure. Boys are socialized into masculinity in a way that limits their ability to access their emotional experience. They aren't taught that they have a 'relationship' with their body that's worth examining, or that they might be vulnerable to pressure and shame around their appearance. We need to change the conversation about body image to acknowledge that boys have relationships with their bodies, food, and exercise as well as girls. We need to normalize their experience of appearance ideals and give them the language and emotional space to process it, in order to help them thrive."

GET SHREDDED—OR NOT?

The one body feature guys seem to complain about most is the size of their muscles. There are a lot of messages in popular culture that suggest to boys and men that they should work to get big muscles, or "get shredded." We are here to tell you that your muscles do not make you a man.

If you are self-conscious about your muscles, realize that there are many reasons for this. Even the Batman action figure you may have played with when you were a little kid had six-pack abs and ridiculously big biceps. In fact, sports scientists have examined action figures that your mom, dad, or grandparents may have played with compared with the ones you probably had as a kid. Guess what? Action figures' muscles have gotten bigger across time. The message to young kids these days seems to be that muscles really matter. Even boys as young as 8 years old say that they are concerned about not having muscles. How many 8-year-old boys have you ever seen who do have muscles? (As you'll see in Chapter 3, it's nearly impossible to develop muscles before puberty.)

Part of the hype about "getting shredded" is not just about building muscles, but losing fat. The ideal male body is often viewed as both lean and muscular. This is a pretty tricky combination for any guy to obtain. Mark Wahlberg (an actor, famous for his roles in *Transformers* in 2014 and

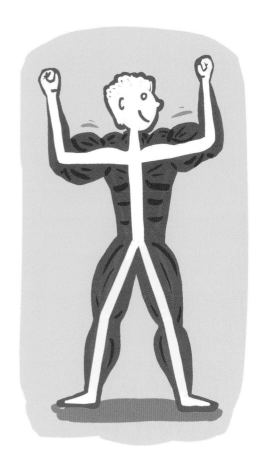

Uncharted in 2021) has admitted that to get the body he has in some of his movies he eats 10–12 meals a day and spends most of the day in the gym. So, while his body may seem impressive, most people can't spare the time that goes into developing it. He also has more money and help (a trainer and a chef) to achieve his goals. If you want to go to school, have a job, or have time for your family and friends, you may need to accept that you will not have a celebrity's shredded body. In fact, most celebrities don't always have the bodies you may find impressive. They follow a difficult eating and exercise regimen for a few months, make a movie, and go back to looking a lot like most people you know.

The **bottom line** is that it is important not to set expectations for yourself that are impossible to achieve. You will only end up feeling disappointed, when in fact no one expects you to look like an action figure, and no one who cares about you does so because of how you look. They care about you for the person that you are and the person you are becoming. As Oliver's story reminds us, it's normal to want to "improve" your body, but you shouldn't ever feel like you need to do this for other people.

MY STORY

OLIVER BENJAMIN, 24 YEARS OLD

I like my body, but at the same time I feel like I have to keep it maintained. Any sign of unwanted fat potentially happening makes me a bit **insecure**. I can also feel insecure about my muscles; I wish my shoulders and biceps were bigger.

When I started college, I realized that I was super-skinny and I wanted to be more like the jocks I saw around me. As a gay, black man, there were many ways that I was not like them, and I was fine with that. But I did admire how fit they looked, and there is definitely an emphasis on looks in gay culture. Fortunately, I learned that I like to exercise. It has boosted my sense of having sex appeal and it's a great stress reliever.

My advice to younger boys would be to try not to feel weighed down by the appearance pressures around you. I appreciate that it's really hard not to be affected, but it's so important to love who you are and to really try to only make changes to your body for yourself and not for anybody else.

BE A MAN AND MAN UP

Has anyone ever told you to "be a man" or "man up"? What do these comments even mean?

If you've heard this before, it likely came up when someone around you—maybe a parent, coach, or friend—felt you should hide your emotions, act tough, or not let others know what you were really thinking. For many years in many cultures, physical strength and emotional quietness have been viewed as "masculine." The messages you and many boys before you have received is that you should not share your thoughts and feelings, and that being a man means being big, strong, and muscular.

This is a very simple and inaccurate view of masculinity. It is also incredibly unfortunate, because this view suggests that what you show on the outside is a really important part of who you are, while everything going on inside your mind is not that important. To be a well-adjusted person, it's important that you nurture all aspects of who you are, including your physical health, psychological well-being, and social connections with other people.

What should you do if your friends tease you about your looks?

Being teased about how you look can be incredibly painful—even if the people teasing you love you and are just joking around. A lot of people who develop low self-esteem and **eating disorders** report that they were once teased about their looks. It's important that you don't let some insulting and hurtful things that other people say rob you of your sense of self. No one looks perfect and we all have body parts that we don't like completely. It's OK to tell your friends that you find their comments hurtful (or not helpful). Your friends are likely to respect you if you tell them to lay off, or cut it out, if they tease you. If your friends don't listen to you, you may want to talk to an adult about this. It's also good to remind yourself that some of our "imperfections" make us unique. They make us who we are and we don't want to totally change them.

TEASING, BULLYING, AND BELONGING

Pretty much everyone cares about being accepted by others. It's human nature to want to form social connections and to feel like we fit in. This may lead you to feel like you belong more in some places than others. Hopefully, you feel like you are loved and cherished by your family. Hopefully, you feel like you have a group of friends. Hopefully, you find yourself in other settings—on sports teams, in a band, or on a debate team—where you feel connected with others. (We'll explain more about the importance of social connections in Chapter 9.)

Not everyone feels like they fit in at home, school, or in any setting. Being teased makes it difficult to feel accepted, and one of the qualities that guys report being teased about more than anything else is their appearance. Maybe you have obviously large feet and your friends call you "big foot," or you have red hair and your friends call you "ginger." It's possible that teasing is how you relate with some of the people in your life, but this doesn't mean you have to like it.

It can be extra hard to appreciate and accept your looks if you feel that other people don't appreciate and accept how you look. In particular, if someone you really care about teases you about a part of your appearance that you are already uncomfortable with, this may lead you to feel terrible. Both overweight and underweight boys report being teased about their weight. In contrast, boys who report having positive experiences with their peers later say that they feel less ashamed and more positively about their bodies.

You can't control all of your interactions with the people around you, and you can't necessarily stop other people from teasing you, but you can change how you react to this teasing. It's a good idea to tell people if they're upsetting you. Your brother, your friend, or whoever is teasing you may not even mean anything by it; maybe they think you understand that they are joking (people can have a strange way of showing that they care about you). You can also choose not to internalize what they say. Internalizing means taking information that's outside of you and making it your own. If your brother tells you that your nose is too big, you can choose to ignore him or you can make his opinion your own opinion, and start to believe your nose is too big. But you don't have to share his (or anyone else's) opinion about your appearance.

Sometimes people can take teasing too far. Someone may even bully you about your appearance or physical self. If someone says something mean, inappropriate, or sexual about your appearance, it is harassment. When a guy experiences bullying or harassment, sometimes he is embarrassed to tell anyone what happened. He may feel angry and upset, but he doesn't always say something to an adult or authority figure. **It's important that you speak up if you ever find yourself in this situation.** Even if you aren't sure how to describe what happened to you, talk to an adult you trust as soon as possible. It may make sense to talk to a teacher, school counselor, coach, or principal if this happens at school. You do not have to experience your negative feelings all on your own. A parent or other trusted adult can help you figure out the best way to handle your experience. And keep in mind that you're doing this for yourself, but also to protect other people who may be bullied or harassed if you don't speak up.

MYTHS & MISBELIEFS

You can either be bullied or be the bully. You have to choose.

Bullying is referred to as a public health problem. Psychologists do not view it as normal or acceptable, even though it is common. Bullying is most common among kids who are about 10–13 years old, followed by slightly older kids (14–18 years old), with one in five kids in this age range in the USA reporting having been bullied at school. The rates are even higher for **cyberbullying** (bullying that takes place online). If you have ever felt bullied about your appearance—or about anything at all—you are not alone! This does not mean that your only option is to become the bully and pick on other people, however.

Research suggests that both those who are bullied *and* those who are bullies experience long-term negative physical and mental consequences. For example, kids who fall into the category of bully or bullied (and some fall into both categories) are more likely to experience **depression**, anxiety, a fear of going to school, sleep difficulties, poor school performance, and substance use and abuse. (See Chapter 9 for more information about depression, anxiety, and substance use, such as alcohol and drug use.) No one wins as far as bullying is concerned.

Fortunately, many schools and communities understand the enormous problem that bullying has become among young people. Anti-bullying programs have been developed and they show that one of the best ways to reduce bullying is to get young people involved in activities they care about, such as a team sport, and to connect them with caring adults or mentors. Even if your school or community does not have an anti-bullying program, you can look for an activity to get involved in and find a teacher, coach, uncle, family friend, or other caring adult to talk with whenever you encounter stress.

SELF-COMPASSION

Sometimes people bully themselves. In other words, some people think about and treat themselves worse than they would treat a friend. We may think that we're too short or too chubby or not athletic enough. We wouldn't tell our friends that we think they're too short or too chubby or not athletic enough, so why do we "talk down" to ourselves like this?

EXPERT ADVICE

Adam Fare, eating disorders **activist**, UK

"We cannot make changes from a place of shame. Shame freezes us. Shame keeps us stuck. Shame takes away our power. Self-compassion is the antidote for toxic shame."

There is evidence that people *think* they benefit from being hard on themselves. They think they'll improve themselves if they bully themselves. However, people tend to benefit more from **self-compassion**. Self-compassion is basically being kind to yourself and treating yourself like you would treat a friend. Scientists have found that people who are self-compassionate tend to experience success because they don't waste energy getting upset with themselves; instead, they focus this energy toward **motivating** themselves to achieve **self-acceptance** and success.

The next time you want to tell yourself that you're out of shape or unattractive, take a deep breath. Remember, this isn't a good use of your energy. Think of a close friend. You're as deserving as your friend, so don't say anything to yourself that you wouldn't say to a close friend. If you're having a hard time feeling accepting of yourself, go back to that mental list we suggested that you make earlier in this chapter and try to focus on your strengths.

BODY CONFIDENCE

It's OK if you sometimes have a hard time feeling good about yourself. It's important to work at this so you can live a happy life. It is expecting a lot of ourselves, however, to think we should feel good *all* the time. In terms of our bodies and our physical appearance, some body image scientists have suggested that we should aim for **body neutrality**. Body neutrality means that we don't dislike our bodies, but we don't put pressure on ourselves to love them all the time either. According to this approach, respecting and caring for our bodies is more important than loving them all the time. It's also important not to spend too much energy thinking about our bodies and appearances.

Of course, body neutrality wasn't really invented with teenagers in mind. So much about being a teenager involves how you fit in with the people around you, and it's normal to have concerns about how others perceive you and whether or not you're "cool." A bit of confidence can go far in the world of teenagers. **Confidence** means that you appreciate your abilities and strengths. Confidence can be genuine and rooted in a deep sense of knowing yourself. Or you can project confidence and try to convince others (and yourself) of your strengths. It's OK to "fake it until you make it" and just work on body neutrality; confidence can come later.

SPENDING TIME ON YOURSELF AND HYGIENE

One change that may signal to you and the people around you that you're growing up is that you'll sweat and smell more than you used to. (See Chapter 3 for more information about puberty.) Good hygiene practices—showering, washing and brushing your hair, wearing deodorant—become especially important during your teen years.

Although it is totally normal to spend time and mental energy on hygiene and **grooming**, you shouldn't spend too much time with thoughts that are related to your body. We think the definition of "**adaptive appearance investment**" is useful for thinking about what is good and what is too far when it comes to caring about our appearance. Adaptive appearance investment is defined as

"regularly engaging in appearance-related self-care, such as grooming behaviors that protect an individual's sense of style and personality; it's enhancing one's natural features via benign (not harmful) methods." According to this definition of what's good or healthy when it comes to caring about our appearance, it's fine to buy clothes that we like and that we think look good on us. It's OK to take time to style our hair. But it's probably unhealthy or risky to do things that pose some danger to you, like spending so much time exercising that you don't have time to do other important activities (like getting enough sleep), or putting your health at risk by using supplements (see Chapter 6 for more on the dangers associated with supplement use).

Even scientists who study body image issues admit that it can be hard to know what is "healthy" caring about your appearance and what is "unhealthy." If

you're worried about how much you care about your appearance, try to spend some time on activities that are not appearance focused. Hopefully, some of the ideas in this book will be useful. It may also be useful to talk to someone about your concerns. The National Eating Disorder Association has a list of counselors on their web page who are trained to help people deal with issues including but also beyond eating disorders, including concerns about appearance, weight, and body image. You may want to check that out.

As you grow up, you'll need to figure out what makes sense for you and how much you want to invest in your appearance, both in terms of money and time. But never forget that the people who care about and love you will not think any differently of you if you have big biceps or no biceps, or if you wear nice clothes or just comfy clothes.

LEVI JAYDEN, 19 YEARS OLD

The relationship I have with my body has always been complicated, as I'm sure it is for most people. I've always viewed my body as something very separate from myself, something that wasn't mine. Obviously, being trans has impacted that. Having a disconnect between how my brain thinks my body should be and how it is biologically is distressing. I started socially and medically transitioning at a relatively young age, which helped bridge that brain-body gap.

I used to and still do struggle with feeling less than other guys. There is a lot of pressure on being one kind of man, which I don't necessarily fit. I'm short and not the most built guy. Despite that, overall, I am at a moment of semi-peace with my body and myself. I've realized that there will always be things about my body that make me uncomfortable and that I strongly dislike, and most of those things aren't within my control. I've found it helpful to adopt a mindset of not worrying about my body because if it's something I can change, I'll change it, and if it isn't, then there's nothing I can do about it but try my best to make peace with it. I can always work out more and build more muscle or lose weight, but I'll never be able to make myself taller or change other structural parts of my body. That shift has helped me come to terms with the things I dislike about my body. However, that is always easier said than done.

When I was younger, I was super-active and played pretty much every sport under the sun—basketball, soccer, baseball, ice hockey, martial arts, and track and field. I played sports because I enjoyed them and also enjoyed being in shape. Sports were a way for me to be proud of my body and physical abilities in a way that was more skill-based rather than appearance-based. I also felt like sports were an equalizer and a way to earn my (male) peers' respect. I stopped playing team sports after middle school, which was about a year after I came out. I really missed being in an athletic space, but there wasn't a space I could be in that early in my transition.

continued ...

In addition to not being allowed to play on either team, it was also a rough space to be in regard to my own body image. It was difficult for me to exercise due to my **dysphoria**. I needed to bind (wear chest compression garments) in order to even really sit in my own skin, which is a very uncomfortable experience. Binding makes anything requiring increased breathing painful, and borderline unsafe. I still enjoyed and felt the need to do something physical outside of team sports so I switched to more independent sports and exercises I could do on my own and outside a gym.

My medical transition has really helped me change the way I feel about my body. After having **top surgery**, I was able to feel more at home in my own skin for the first time in my life. It lifted a huge mental weight, and I could finally stop feeling so "at war" with my body. It also allowed me to go back to being active and involved in sports in a way that wasn't harming my body (by binding).

It may sound like a cliché, but the internet and **social media** have had a really significant impact on my body image, both in negative and positive ways. There's a lot of imagery now with more diverse body types and types of men, but overall, and when I was younger, it was mostly a lot of messaging that there was one way to be a man (from a physical/body standpoint). This messaging makes things complicated and brings on feelings of inadequacy when you don't by default fit any of those images.

If I was to offer advice to younger guys, I'd say to try and find the positives about your body, even if it's just one small thing you like about it. It's very easy to get stuck in the "I hate everything about my body" rabbit hole, but finding even one thing can help stop that spiral. I've also found it helpful to focus on the positive aspects of your appearance, and the non-appearance-based things you like about what your body can do, whether it's that you're super-good at climbing trees, or throwing a ball, or running—just something more skill-based, rather than appearance-based.

One of my good friends is really popular and good-looking. Girls love him. I like hanging out with him, because I get more attention from girls when I'm with him. I also feel a bit jealous of him. I don't want to feel jealous of my friend and I don't want him to feel like I'm using him to get girls' attention. What should I do?

It can be very difficult to feel like you don't measure up or aren't as popular as a friend. Most of us feel this way at some time. This may be a good situation to practice not comparing yourself to others. Psychologists refer to this as social comparison, and rarely does anything good come of comparing your appearance to that of others. In fact, research suggests that people tend to feel bad about themselves when they engage in this kind of social comparison.

It's easy to look at someone else's life and feel like it's better than your own, but that's usually because we make social comparisons on just one aspect of life. It may seem like someone else has a better life because he receives more attention from girls. However, maybe he doesn't do as well in school, or isn't as good at sports as you are. Each of us has our own strengths, whether in terms of our ability to make friends, our athleticism, or our sense of humor. Focus on your strengths and try to be happy for other people when they have success on the basketball court or with a new girlfriend.

Finally, it probably hasn't occurred to your friend that you are using his friendship to attract girls. If you aren't doing this—and you really enjoy being his friend—then you have nothing to worry about. Your friend may like you because you can help him with his math homework or you always make him laugh. You may like him because he's fun to play soccer with and he has a lot of friends that are girls. Everyone brings different assets to their relationships and they don't have to be the same.

IT'S OK TO CARE ABOUT HOW YOU LOOK

Caring about your appearance is a complex thing. To review what we've covered so far: don't let others make you feel bad about your appearance, and treat yourself with kindness. Take care of yourself and practice good hygiene, but it's also OK to aim for body neutrality, or not thinking too much about your appearance. This doesn't mean that you need to totally ignore how you look. The take-home message from this book is *not* that you need to stop caring about how you look.

Did you know that worldwide, people spend *$382 billion* each year on perfumes, cosmetics, and toiletries? In one recent survey in the UK, men reported spending about the same amount of money and time grooming themselves (showering, shaving, choosing clothes, styling their hair) as women did. Spending time and money to make ourselves look and smell nice is important to many people, because this reveals that we care about ourselves. In fact, psychologists call this self-care (see Chapter 9 for a lot more about self-care). There is absolutely nothing wrong with taking good care of ourselves, whether that is taking time to wash and style our hair or selecting clothes that we like.

However, if you spend a lot of time looking in the mirror and worrying about your appearance, you may care a bit *too* much. The average man spends about 30 minutes on his appearance each day. Spending too much more than that could cut into the time you can spend on homework, friendship, hobbies, and even sleep. It is important to balance investing in yourself and your appearance so you feel confident and well groomed with spending more time on the other important aspects of your life. Others are not likely to notice a lot of the things that we notice about ourselves. A pimple that is bothering you or a bad haircut are both likely to go unnoticed by others.

You can choose to pay less attention to some details of your appearance and focus that time and energy on other aspects of your life.

REMEMBER: THIS MATTERS —A LOT!

Focusing on the positive and working toward a positive body image is very important. A big part of this is developing **healthy** habits, such as good eating habits (see Chapter 6 for more about healthy eating). Loving your body isn't just a superficial concern. It's not just about loving how you look. Feeling good about your body and taking care of it is important to your health, how you view yourself, and how you view the rest of the world. It's worth investing time in yourself and working on *learning* to love your body if you don't already. You only get one body to last your entire lifetime. It's important that you're good to yourself!

Summing Up #LoveYourselfFirst

- ☑ Get into the habit of focusing on the parts of your body that you like, and not the parts that you dislike.
- ☑ Think of the ways your body helps you—running, eating, sleeping, and laughing—and be as kind to yourself as you would be to a friend.
- ☑ Take good care of yourself and work toward maintaining good hygiene habits without spending too much time or energy worrying about your appearance.

Find out more

- For more information about bullying and helpful suggestions, check out this web page: www.stopbullying.gov/resources/get-help-now.
- The **Centers for Disease Control and Prevention** has information about bullying and prevention on its web page as well: www.cdc.gov/injury/features/stop-bullying/index.html.
- The National Eating Disorder Association has a list of counselors on their web page who are trained to help people cope with eating and body image issues: www.nationaleatingdisorders.org/find-treatment/treatment-and-support-groups.
- For more scholarly articles and web pages with information about body image, see the companion website to this book: www.theBodyImageBookforBoys.com.

CHAPTER THREE

WHAT THE HECK IS GOING ON?

#ThisIsJustTheBeginning

"WE CANNOT BECOME WHAT WE WANT BY REMAINING WHAT WE ARE."

Max De Pree, American businessman and writer

WHAT IS PUBERTY?

We're sure you've heard the word puberty, but maybe you aren't sure exactly what it means. The word puberty comes from the Latin word *pubescere*, which means "to grow hairy." You probably already know (and maybe you've already experienced for yourself) that growing up does include getting hairier, but there's more to it than that. Puberty is the end of childhood and the beginning of a tremendous amount of physical and psychological growth. All of this change may seem strange at times, but it is also really exciting.

In this chapter you'll learn

- ○ about the changes you will experience during puberty,
- ○ how puberty may affect your body image, and
- ○ how to cope with the physical changes you experience during puberty and keep a positive view of yourself.

WHAT CHANGES DURING PUBERTY?

Skin

You've probably noticed that as kids become teenagers, they sometimes get pimples, or spots. This is related to changes in your skin that all teens experience. It's normal for your skin to get rougher and dryer in some places, and oilier in other places. This oiliness may lead you to break out and develop red bumps and patches on your skin, especially on your face, chest, and back. Pimples, or spots, can be a cause for concern and self-consciousness among teens, but in most cases they disappear on their own and they can be treated. Help your skin by washing with a soap specifically intended for your face. This kind of soap can be found in nearly any drugstore or grocery store. If you have pimples, you may also want to treat them with a cream that contains salicylic

acid or **benzoyl peroxide**. If this doesn't help, you can ask your doctor (perhaps a **pediatrician** or a **dermatologist**, a doctor who specializes in skin care) for a more powerful skin treatment. There are many effective treatments for pimples and **acne**.

Changes in your skin also lead to more sweating and the potential for **body odor** (BO), as C.V.'s story describes. Showering and washing well with soap can help with BO. Most of the sweat occurs under your arms, and deodorant can greatly reduce the likelihood of smelling bad. If you don't like the smell of one particular deodorant, or it doesn't seem to work for you, then try another kind. There are dozens of options to consider. You may be tempted to try to cover up BO with cologne or "body spray." This doesn't usually work and can actually leave you smelling worse; you're much better off jumping in the shower.

One final change to your skin that you may notice is **stretch marks**. Stretch marks will appear as "stripes" of skin colored a bit differently from the rest of your skin. They can occur anywhere as a result of rapid growth, are a normal occurrence during puberty, and may fade with time.

MY STORY

C.V. THOMAS, 13 YEARS OLD

I'd say that I'm generally okay with my body. I might look better if I lost a pound or two, but I don't think that I really need to.

I probably started to think about my body a bit differently when I was about 11 years old. I noticed that I started to smell a lot more then. I know that's normal and stuff, but it was still sorta weird.

My parents have definitely had an impact on how I feel about myself. Because of them I know that no two bodies are going to be the same and you really have no choice but to just be yourself. Knowing this makes growing up a little easier.

MYTHS & MISBELIEFS

> Eating chocolate can cause you to break out.

It seems pretty unfair that something as delicious as chocolate could make you break out in spots or pimples. Fortunately, this is mostly a myth. I say "mostly" because scientists have found that what you eat can affect your skin. Eating **healthy** foods, including plenty of fruits and vegetables, can help your skin look healthier and prevent **breakouts**. Avoid eating a lot of **sugar** and simple **carbohydrates** ("carbs," found in white bread and other **processed foods** like chips, or crisps) because these foods can increase the risk of getting **acne**. Acne is caused by the many changes occurring in the body during **adolescence**, so a healthy diet still may not prevent acne.

Hair

Hair creeps up in all sorts of places when you go through puberty. This may be one of the first things you notice when you begin puberty. It may begin with a few hairs under your arms, or **pubic hair**, or more hair on your legs or on your face. Your hair also gets thicker and darker. Some of this new hair may be the same color as the hair on your head, but some may be a different color.

Boys and men often remove some of this newly appearing hair, especially on their face, but you do not have to do this. There are no health reasons for removing body hair—it is completely natural and normal. Facial hair is likely to get darker and thicker over time, so you may notice some facial hair in your teens, but it may not be enough that you want to do anything about it until your 20s. Talk to a man you trust about hair removal; a father or uncle has probably been looking forward to showing you

how to **shave**. Of course, there are also videos on YouTube that can show you what you need to know to make sure you don't cut yourself.

Some men remove some of their body hair, for example on their chest or back. Two of the most common ways to do this are shaving and waxing. Waxing usually involves a trip to a salon where a professional applies hot wax to unwanted hair, allows the wax to cool and harden, and then pulls the wax off removing the underlying hair at the same time. Keep in mind that a desire to get rid of hair probably comes from what you've learned from the people and **media** around you. In some cultures, hair removal isn't expected and no one does it. Before you pursue any sort of hair removal, make sure that you have the supplies and the help you may need. Don't feel overwhelmed if you look for shaving supplies and find a lot of options such as creams, gels, and different sorts of razor blades; you'll figure out what you like and what works for you over time.

Voice

As you become a teenager, it is typical for your voice to change. Your voice will start to sound lower and deeper because your vocal cords and voice box grow. Your voice may not change all at once, but may go through a period when sometimes it sounds higher and other times it sounds lower. Some of the change may be so gradual that you don't notice it at all, or the change may be fast enough that you do notice it. Don't worry if your voice sounds squeaky sometimes—that is totally normal, too. When your voice box grows, you may actually be able to see changes in your throat. The bump it forms in your throat is sometimes called an Adam's apple.

Q+A

Hair is starting to grow on my upper lip. It is not super-dark or thick, but it bothers me and I think it looks weird. I don't have hair on the rest of my face yet. Can I shave just my mustache hair?

It is typical to start to grow hair on your upper lip (your mustache) before you grow hair on the rest of your face. It is also possible to shave this hair even before you grow any hair elsewhere. It is not necessary or important to shave for health reasons, so shave only if you find the hair bothersome to you. Some boys start to shave as young as 10 or 11 years of age and some don't start until they are in their 20s.

It is possible to shave with an electric razor or a razor blade (which may be a disposable or cartridge razor). An electric razor may be easiest if you are only trying to remove a bit of fuzzy hair, as it does not need to be used with shaving cream and your chances of cutting yourself are lower than with a razor blade. Some guys prefer to use a razor blade because they feel this provides a closer, smoother shave. If you are going to use a razor blade, it's usually best to use shaving cream or soap on your face as this helps to protect your face. It is also typically best to shave in the same direction that the hair grows. For most guys, this means shaving downward where their mustache is and along their sideburns. You may find that the hair on your neck and the lower part of your face grows upwards, so switch directions to shave those areas.

Some boys and men like to just rinse their face with some cool water when they have finished shaving and some like to use aftershave lotion. Some lotions may smell nice, but might be irritating to your skin. You may want to check with someone you trust about products that have a strong scent; what smells nice to you may not smell nice to others.

Bones, heart, and lungs

Even body parts that don't seem related to puberty are affected by it. For example, your bones grow in length (how do you think you get taller?) and they become thicker. Your skeleton will be about twice the weight at the end of puberty as you grow taller and your bones become stronger. Your heart nearly doubles in size over the course of puberty. This

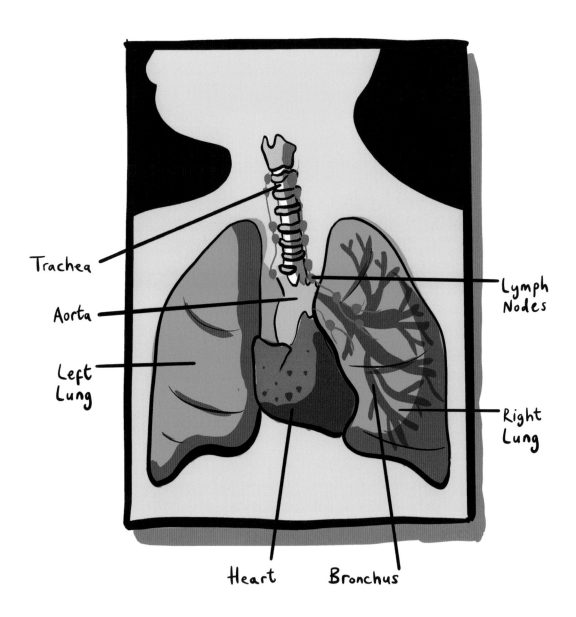

Trachea

Aorta

Left
Lung

Lymph
Nodes

Right
Lung

Heart   Bronchus

EXPERT ADVICE

Dr. Cara Natterson, MD, author of *Guy Stuff* and *The Care and Keeping of You*, USA

"Since I am a doctor, kids often share their worries about puberty with me. This gives me a pretty clear picture of how normal it is to wonder what is going to happen, when, and how much. Want to know how tall you are going to be? How **muscular**? Or how hairy? I wish I could tell you, but I can't—no one can. But doctors can reassure you that something you might be **stressed** about is completely normal—and if it's not, doctors can help you figure out what's going on."

allows your heart to beat more slowly while still pumping blood as well as it did when you were younger. Your lungs get much larger, which allows oxygen to move through your body more effectively. Overall, these physical changes can make you taller, bigger, and stronger. They can even make you more capable of doing well at a variety of sports.

Height

Before puberty, you probably grew at least an inch (or around 2.5 cm) taller each year. During puberty, however, you are likely to experience a **growth spurt** and grow 2–4 inches per year for a few years. Every boy is different, so it is impossible to be sure when this will happen. Your growth spurt could start before you become an official teenager and it may not end until you are in your 20s.

How tall you grow is controlled by biology and genes. Stretching won't make you taller, nor will exercise; and most likely your eating habits won't matter. A balanced diet (see more about protein and healthy food choices in Chapter 6) ensures that you will grow to the height determined by your biology and genes.

You are likely to notice that girls seem to grow taller and experience a growth spurt before boys do. This is because girls tend to start puberty about 2 years before boys do. Most girls will begin their growth spurt in middle school (10–13 years old, approximately) before boys experience their growth spurt. Don't worry—you will catch up with the girls in a few years!

Weight and muscles

It's important for you to know that you will gain weight and muscles during puberty, and your body shape will change. This is totally normal. Everything about you is getting bigger, even your heart. Plus, as we mentioned above, you're probably going to be several inches taller at the end of puberty. It's completely normal for you to have broader shoulders and longer arms and legs. Most boys like how their bodies change during puberty, but not all do. Sometimes it just takes a while to get used to your new body.

Most boys appreciate that their bodies become more adult-looking during puberty. However, physical development occurs gradually over puberty, and sometimes there are phases when changes occur only to reverse months later. For example, you may notice that your breasts grow a bit, temporarily, before you experience muscle growth in your chest. You may notice that your hands and feet have grown a lot, but nothing else about you seems to have changed. You may grow taller long before you grow stronger. This is all totally normal.

If you find yourself feeling upset about how your body has changed, it's a good idea to talk to someone about your concerns. If you are too uncomfortable to talk with your friends, who will be having similar experiences, talk to a parent or another adult that you trust. If you feel like you want to talk with an expert, your doctor, school nurse or counselor, or a therapist can be very helpful. Remember that puberty is a process that everyone goes through and most people experience some of it as awkward, and that is perfectly normal.

I've started to work out in the school gym with my football team. However, my muscles don't seem any bigger after months of this. One of the older guys on my team told me that I'd need **steroids** to ever bulk up. Are steroids safe?

The easy answer to this question is: NO!

Our bodies produce natural steroids, which are hormones that help to promote growth and development. Anabolic steroids are an unnatural version of steroids that can be taken as pills or injected into the body. They are illegal unless prescribed by a physician, and their use is not allowed among professional athletes.

Steroids *may* increase muscle size, but their use also can be *really bad* for your health. Steroids can shrink your testicles, thicken breast tissue, cause mood swings and even depression, and stop you from growing taller. Steroid use is also associated with minor issues such as hair loss, oily hair, and acne, as well as really serious issues such as heart attacks and cancer. Anabolic steroid use can become addictive, meaning it can be difficult to stop taking steroids once a person starts.

Given all the really serious risks associated with steroid use, no one should ever use them, but teenagers especially should avoid them given the risks associated with growth and development. If you know anyone who has tried steroids and needs help to stop, encourage them to talk to a doctor or other professional.

Many people probably wish that they could take a pill to look how they'd like to look. It's easy to see why some would be tempted to take steroids so that they could become more muscular. If you feel tempted to try steroids, however, you should talk to someone like a parent, brother or sister, or school counselor. Feeling really concerned about your appearance is stressful and is not something you need to deal with alone. Keep reading this book, but don't be afraid to seek out the social support you need from the people around you.

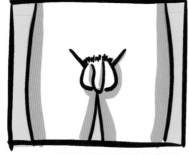

Genitals

Your **genitals**—penis, **testicles** (aka "balls"), and **scrotum** (the sac that holds your testicles)—will also change during puberty. Some of the changes are hidden by the growth of pubic hair that will cover some of your genital area, and some of the changes will happen so gradually that you may not notice them. The first change is likely to be the growth of your testicles. Gradually, your penis will start to grow, first in length and then also in width. Your scrotum will likely change in color and look darker by the end of puberty.

The figure shows the five stages of genital development, which are often called "Tanner stages" after the doctor (James Tanner) who first described them. These stages are used by doctors and researchers to characterize the extent of pubertal development. In other words, they show the typical steps of genital development. Notice that there are no ages associated with these stages—just an ordering of what comes first, then second, and so on—because these stages occur at very different ages for different people. (There are also five stages of development for girls.)

EXPERT ADVICE

Professor Gemma Sharp, PhD, *Monash University, Australia*

"I would like boys and men to know that size doesn't matter! Having a larger penis does not make someone more of a man. Being a man is far more than anatomy. It's about being a whole person who is allowed to have a range of thoughts and feelings."

I'm worried that my penis doesn't look normal and hasn't grown very much. How can I tell what is "normal" and does the size of your penis matter?

Probably most boys worry about the appearance of their penis and probably no two penises look alike. There is no "normal"-looking penis and boys' penises grow at different ages and rates.

One thing that leads some penises to look different from others is whether or not they are circumcised. Circumcision is the removal of the foreskin that covers the top of the penis. If this is removed, it is usually done in the hospital in the first day or so following a boy's birth or during a religious ceremony when a boy is a baby. Circumcision is not necessary for health and does not alter how the penis functions. In some cultures, circumcision is considered important. The World Health Organization estimates that in most European countries and the UK, fewer than 20% of boys are circumcised, while in the USA, more than 75% of boys are circumcised.

In terms of the size of your penis, some research suggests that almost half of men wish that their penis was larger. Most penises are fairly similar in size, with an average length of around 3.5 inches (9 cm) when they are flaccid (soft) and about 5 inches (13 cm) when they are erect (hard). Although men have been found to feel more confident if they perceive their penis to be larger than average, penis size does not affect penis function. If you have any concerns about the appearance or function of your penis, ask your doctor about this. It may be embarrassing to bring up, but doctors are used to talking about all sorts of embarrassing topics and you are likely to find reassurance from the conversation. Also, the expert advice from Prof. Sharp may be reassuring and comes from her many years of doing research to understand genital body image (which is basically how people feel about the appearance and functioning of their genitals).

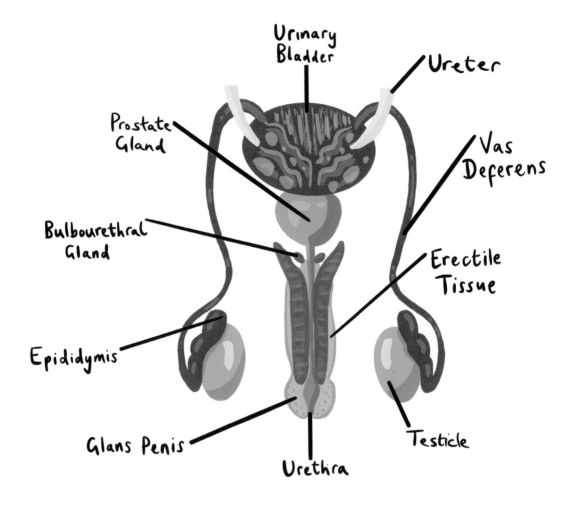

Urinary Bladder

Ureter

Prostate Gland

Vas Deferens

Bulbourethral Gland

Erectile Tissue

Epididymis

Glans Penis

Testicle

Urethra

Ejaculation, erections, and masturbation

The outer appearance of your genitals is not the only thing that changes during puberty. Semenarche, or sperm development, begins in the testes. The only way for you to know that sperm development has begun is when you experience spermarche, or your first ejaculation. Usually, boys experience their first ejaculation of semen, which contains sperm and other fluid, while they are asleep. This is called a nocturnal emission or a wet dream. You may wake up one morning to discover a sticky fluid in your underwear or on your sheets. This may have occurred because you had a dream that led you to experience an erection and then ejaculation. You may not remember having a dream at all. Wet dreams are completely normal and happen to nearly all boys during puberty.

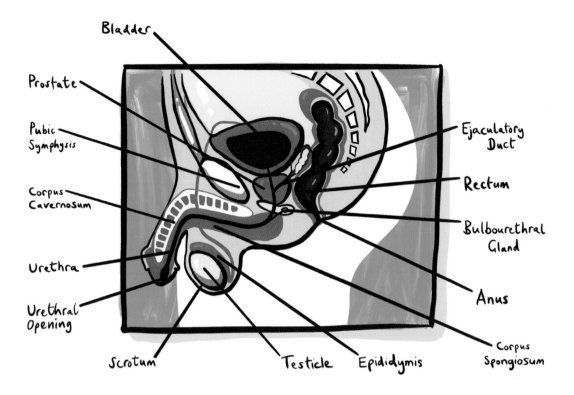

It is also normal during puberty to experience erections while you are awake. Erections occur when blood flows to the penis causing the soft tissue of the penis to grow firm. This may occur because you touch your penis or because you feel excited, nervous, or for no reason at all. Spontaneous erections—those that occur for what seems like no reason at all—have the potential to be embarrassing, even though they are totally normal. If you find yourself at school or in a situation where you do not want to have an erection, the best thing to do is to think about something else (not your penis!) and put a book or sweatshirt over your lap and it will go away fairly quickly.

If you experience an erection in private, it is normal to want to touch your penis. You will find that rubbing your penis will feel good; this is called masturbation (sometimes referred to as "whacking off," "jerking off," and "wanking," as well as many other terms). If you rub your penis for a little while, you are likely to have an orgasm, or ejaculate. Most boys masturbate and there is nothing unhealthy or wrong about doing so. Your body will keep producing more sperm and you are likely to learn about your body and your sexual preferences when you masturbate. You may want to be careful not to get semen somewhere where it cannot easily be removed. Sometimes boys choose to masturbate in the shower to save themselves any trouble with cleaning up afterwards.

MYTHS & MISBELIEFS

Wearing tight-fitting underwear may keep your body from being able to produce sperm.

Most boys will grow up wearing briefs—underwear that is relatively tight fitting. As you get older, you may want to wear boxers—underwear that more closely resembles loose-fitting shorts. You may also want underwear that is a hybrid of these two types, boxer briefs. Choose underwear that is comfortable to you and that you like. However, there are a few things to keep in mind.

First, tight-fitting underwear, or briefs, should not affect your sperm production in any way. If you find this type of underwear to be most comfortable, there is no health reason to avoid wearing it. You may find that certain fabrics are more comfortable and breathable, such as cotton. This matters, regardless of the style of underwear you wear, because you are likely to notice that you sweat more during your teen years than you did as a child. Next, be sure to wash your genital area thoroughly with soap and water when you shower and dry your penis and scrotum before putting underwear on. Finally, don't wear the same pair of underwear for more than 1 day. It is important to adopt good hygiene habits when it comes to your genitals and your underwear so that you don't end up smelling bad.

Hormones

Up until puberty, girls' and boys' levels of a variety of hormones are very similar. This changes during puberty. At puberty, boys' levels of male-specific hormones including testosterone increase dramatically.

Sometimes parents and other adults will say that moodiness during puberty is due to hormone changes. This may be partially true, but it's likely to be an overly simple explanation for a lot of the complicated changes that take place during puberty. For example, it's possible that you may feel hungry soon after eating, or tired despite sleeping a lot, due to changes in your hormones. In turn, hunger and fatigue may make you grouchy. Or maybe you feel stressed because you haven't been getting along with your friends at school and you don't have classes with the people you wish you did. Some of this may be related to your hormones, but a lot of it may not be. The bottom line is that you shouldn't feel like your life is out of control due to hormone changes. Your hormones play a really important role in your development, but they don't control everything.

Testosterone is often discussed in popular culture because of its perceived association with muscle growth, athletic success, and aggression. Although some research suggests that testosterone is associated with aggression, it's not the only hormone that is relevant to aggression. For example, cortisol (a hormone that is released in response to stress among males and females) is also associated with aggressive behavior. In other words, just because your levels of testosterone increase during your teen years, this does not mean that you are likely to become more aggressive. Other personality, biological, and social factors matter a great deal in determining how you behave. Testosterone does not *cause* aggression, nor is it an excuse for aggressive behavior. If you find yourself having a hard time controlling your temper, this is not typical or "manly"; it is a problem that you should talk with someone about. A parent, a school counselor, or your doctor may be able to offer advice or refer you to someone who can help you learn to regulate your emotions.

WHAT'S NORMAL?

What sometimes gets missed in all the discussions of puberty and the physical changes is that every boy is unique. **No two boys' experiences are exactly the same.** If you notice hair on your chest before you notice a growth spurt, that's OK. If you get pimples after you notice a growth spurt, that's OK too. If you're in your early teens and you don't notice much about your body that has changed, there's nothing to stress about. Recent research suggests that the majority of boys will experience most of their pubertal changes between the ages of 11 and 17 years. However, it's not uncommon for boys to notice some signs of puberty as early as 9 or 10 years of age, and it's also perfectly normal for boys not to have completed puberty until they're in their late teens or even their early 20s. The timing of puberty is influenced by biological factors (your genes), diet, and cultural environment. You can't control the timing of puberty, but you can be prepared for the changes that you'll experience. As Drew's story reminds us, you can't skip puberty, and you'll probably spend a lot of time thinking about all of this.

EXPERT ADVICE

Professor Robert Atkins, PhD, and nurse, Rutgers University, USA

"The truest thing I can say about puberty as a man, school nurse, and father is that once you have seen one boy go through puberty you have seen one boy go through puberty. All boys go through it, but characteristics such as the timing, pace of change, and emotional experience vary. For some boys, it seems to happen overnight, and others will still be growing and changing into their early 20s."

MY STORY

DREW STEPHEN, 19 YEARS OLD

I guess I don't think my body is anything particularly outstanding. I actually try not to think too much about it at all!

I think that my feelings about my body changed during the beginning of middle school. By the time I was about 11 years old, I remember thinking that my body was another thing I was thinking about from day to day. Before middle school, I can't remember ever thinking about my body unless I was feeling sick or hurt.

My parents have definitely influenced how I feel about myself and my body, in particular. My parents have always been super-supportive of me and they have made it really clear that the most important thing was to make sure that I was healthy. As long as my doctor approved of my physical shape and health, then I shouldn't be concerned with what others thought.

AFTER YOUR TEENS

For most guys, the completion of puberty doesn't mean that your body stays the same for the rest of your life. There are a variety of things that can affect both the appearance and function of your body. Your weight will likely fluctuate from week to week and year to year. There are a lot of reasons for these fluctuations: changes in eating habits, stress, the amount you **exercise**, how much you sleep, changes in hormones, and even just your age (people tend to gain weight with age, even past puberty). Changes can sometimes make people anxious, but it's healthy to think of your body's ability to adjust and change in so many ways as pretty amazing.

Q+A

How do you know when you're done? And then what happens?

It's not usually obvious when puberty has come to an end for any one boy. Most boys will finish growing taller toward the end of their teen years, but you could be among the minority of boys who grow taller into your 20s. For most boys, the changes discussed in this chapter—hair growth, skin changes, voice changes—will be underway, if not completed by the late teen years. This doesn't mean that your body is done changing for the rest of your life.

If you're like most people, you may gain weight with age and you may lose weight, too. Your skin will show signs of aging (for example, you'll develop wrinkles and freckles or "sun spots"). Parts of your body may sag or you may notice stretch marks (a sort of skin scarring that is a bit of a different color than the rest of your skin due to rapid growth of the skin). This is all totally normal, and it's up to you to decide if you want to embrace getting older or resist it.

HOW IS THIS RELATED TO BODY IMAGE?

Research shows that most boys' understanding of themselves and their body image develops right around the same time that their bodies are changing due to puberty. These changes are likely to affect body image. Some scientists have suggested that because boys tend to become taller and more muscular during puberty, they're also more likely to feel confident about their bodies after puberty. Not every guy grows into a body he likes or feels comfortable with, however, and hardly any boy develops a body that resembles that of Chris Evans' (Captain America) or Dwayne "The Rock" Johnson. Most men's bodies look little like the bodies of famous people you see in movies, on Instagram, and in YouTube videos. It's important to realize that changes to your body are all a normal part of growing up, and how you look is not the most important thing about you.

SELF-ACCEPTANCE

We discuss **self-acceptance** a lot in this book, but it's important to think about it in terms of puberty and the changes that will occur to your body as you age. To some it feels completely natural to grow bigger and mature, while to others, body changes feel strange and even embarrassing. **Remember that it's completely normal for your body to change as you age.** Even if you aren't sure you like all the changes that have occurred, there's nothing to be embarrassed about. There are great books written about puberty for boys that you can find in a library or online. (Be careful not to rely on the internet too much; not all the information online is accurate.) We list some of our favorite books on this topic at the end of this chapter. Consult these books if you have more questions, and don't hesitate to talk with a trusted adult like a father, mother, uncle, teacher, cousin, or even your doctor. Everyone goes through puberty eventually, and everyone has some questions about it, so no one will think any less of you for asking.

Summing Up #ThisIsJustTheBeginning

- ☑ Your body will change in many ways during puberty. Some changes include getting taller, growing stronger bones and lungs, gaining muscle mass, and developing a deeper voice.

- ☑ It's completely normal to experience all the physical changes caused by puberty, but you may not necessarily experience them in the same ways that your friends do, or at the same time.

- ☑ It's important to focus on accepting the physical changes that take place during puberty and to maintain a positive body image. Reach out to trusted adults for guidance about any of the changes that you need help dealing with.

Find out more

- If you're looking for information about puberty and sexual health that is beyond the scope of this chapter, consider checking out *It's Perfectly Normal: Changing Bodies, Growing Up, Sex, and Sexual Health* (2014) by Robie H. Harris and Michael Emberley. Publisher: Candlewick Press. We love the scientific detail and honesty in Robie Harris' books about growing up and you will, too.

- There are a lot of good books about puberty, but two of our favorites are: *Guy Stuff: The Body Book for Boys* (2017) by Cara Natterson. Publisher: American Girl Publishing; and *The Boy's Body Book: Everything You Need to Know for Growing Up You!* (2015) by Kelli Dunham. Publisher: Appleseed Press. These books answer many of the questions you and boys your age typically have about puberty.

- Many books about puberty can be found in your local library, but don't be afraid to ask an adult to purchase these for you. Most adults are relieved when the kids in their lives want to read about topics they may find difficult to discuss.

- For more scholarly articles and reliable web pages with information about puberty, see the companion website for this book: www.TheBodyImageBookforBoys.com.

CHAPTER FOUR

YOUR IMAGE

#BeYourOwnInfluencer

> "BE YOURSELF. EVERYONE
> ELSE IS ALREADY TAKEN."
>
> Oscar Wilde, Irish poet
> and playwright

What do you notice about all the guys you see on YouTube, Instagram, TikTok, television, and other forms of media? They probably *look* perfect to you, but in fact they're regular people made to look "perfect" through the magic of cosmetics and technology.

In this chapter you'll learn

○ how the media makes ordinary people look anything but ordinary,

○ the role that social media may play in your body image and how to become media literate, and

○ the importance of being thoughtful about self-acceptance when making appearance-related choices.

IT'S JUST NOT "REAL"

Have you ever played with a filter on your phone or computer to change how a picture looks? Tweaked a selfie so you look a little better? Maybe you've done this plenty of times. You've cropped a tree out of a picture or made a colored picture black and white. Now, imagine that you could hand your pictures over to a professional photographer. In fact, imagine that the professional photographer took the pictures in the first place and is going to edit them for you with all the latest software. Your hair will look smoother, your skin will look clearer, and your eyes will look brighter. Maybe your shoulders will look broader, your legs longer, and your biceps bigger.

EXPERT ADVICE

Jaclyn Siegel, PhD, *social psychologist and body image researcher, USA*

"Body ideals are just as **unrealistic** and **unobtainable** for men as they are for women. The 'ideal' body for men is extremely lean and muscular, and boys and men sometimes try to meet this impossible ideal by engaging in disordered eating or excessive exercise."

This is the story behind the photographs posted
by celebrities and people who have a big following
on social media (aka **influencers**). We've talked
with professional photographers in the process of
doing our research, and they all tell us the same
thing: every photo and video is edited. People who
are good-looking to start with end up being extra
handsome as a result of computer editing. When
you look at famous people online or in magazines or
movies, you don't see what they really look like.

Why are all the pictures edited? The answer is
obvious: who doesn't want a pimple edited away, or
a stray hair removed? Unfortunately, the result of all
this editing is that we come to believe that there are

lots of real people who are physically perfect. This isn't true. Everyone—everyone!—has imperfections.

Movies and videos are edited and staged, as well. There's lighting, video filters, and professional make-up artists (yup, even for guys). There are **stylists** and editors who can do all sorts of things to change the way a person looks. Off-screen, celebrities and influencers can change their appearance using other means such as cosmetic surgery (and other **enhancements** like hair coloring and styling; more on all of that later in this chapter). The main point is this: what you see is not reality. Because these images aren't accurate, you shouldn't compare yourself to them. As Lucas says in his story below, "The modern perfect body is fake!"

The images you see are **manipulated** for another reason, too: they're usually intended to sell you a product or a service. Sometimes you're being sold the idea that physical perfection is possible. Celebrities and influencers appear on social media looking perfect to sell everything from clothes to athletic equipment. That new energy drink that you think you *need* now—where did you first see it? Was it an ad on YouTube? A TikTok post by an influencer? Companies provide social media and apps for free in order to sell you stuff (they don't charge you; they earn money through advertising instead).

LUCAS MICHAEL, 21 YEARS OLD

I have mixed feelings about my body. Some days I'm happy with it and feel comfortable with the fact that the only body I have is a decent one. Other days, I look in the mirror and wish something or other was different. As I become older, these negative thoughts are becoming less and less frequent as I come to terms with the fact that this bit of meat is mine for life!

I do care about what I eat, but not necessarily enough to change anything about my (imperfect) habits. I would like to be a healthy eater and I definitely feel better about myself when I've had a healthy meal, but as a student (at the University of Sussex), it's sometimes hard to eat well. I've always had a high metabolism and I've always been pretty active. However, during the coronavirus pandemic, I started to be more self-conscious as I was way less active and eating a lot more snacks and noticed a little more belly on me.

I love skateboarding and tennis purely because of the happiness they bring to me, although I like to feel like I've done my body some good at the end of the day and got my heart pumping. However, I also work out at home with weights and do abs and stuff. I would say this is purely for aesthetic reasons, although sometimes it's enjoyable. Mostly, I just do this because I don't want to have skinny arms and would prefer to see myself as sexy as opposed to skinny.

I'm probably more self-conscious about my body hair than I am about my arms, though. I remember in school we had swimming lessons when I was about 14, and none of the other boys had any real body hair, but I had hairy legs, arms and even a little on my chest. Being different than everyone else definitely made me self-conscious, as it drew unwanted attention to my body. It's also going to sound silly, but once I read a tweet from this girl I barely knew who said something along the lines of "How could anyone find hairy chests attractive?" Having a very hairy chest myself, that really stuck

continued ...

with me. This must have been 3 years ago, but I still remember the girl and the tweet. Even though my girlfriend says she likes it, so it shouldn't matter what others think, I'm still conscious of the fact that many people think it's ugly, which makes it more uncomfortable to be around people shirtless, as I don't know which side they're on! You never see hairy guys on TV or social media! Just ads for "manscaping" razors or wax strips. All of this sends me the message that my body hair is ugly.

I want young people to realize that everything they see nowadays is a lie! What I mean by this is that we are bombarded by "sexy" people with their "perfect" bodies and the women are always wearing make-up or have gotten **Botox** or fake eyelashes, fake nails, fake boobs, fake everything! The modern perfect body is fake. I think it's wrong. Personally, I like the natural look. I think the key to a good body is just to be healthy, but for your own sake. It's good to feel good, but this comes from within. If you compare yourselves to others and to society's beauty standards, then you're always going to want more and to want to be "better," but you'll never actually reach that. I know stunning girls who just want to be like a girl who is even more stunning. No one is happy these days. The expectations are unnatural, and I just wish everyone would take a step back and say, "Hey, we are all actually pretty beautiful already." I really wish society put less importance on beauty and a bit more on real things like emotions and how we treat each other. Life is not a beauty contest.

YOU'RE SMART ENOUGH NOT TO BE FOOLED, RIGHT?

We like to think that we're unaffected by advertising. We know that people are trying to sell us products, so we believe we can escape the influence. The problem, though, is that you see so very many advertisements each day, in so many different forms of media, that it's virtually impossible to tune them all out.

Researchers who study how the media contributes to body image have found, across many different studies, that the media *does* affect body image. The media presents an unrealistic ideal of perfection that affects us all. In particular, seeing "perfected" and photoshopped images of guys' bodies has a negative impact on boys' (and men's) feelings about their bodies, and their feelings in general. What this means is that looking at these sorts of images tends to make boys think, "I wish I looked like that" and "I don't like how I look, because I'd rather look like that." Boys may also may feel insecure, sad, or anxious as a result of seeing these images.

A big part of the reason you may feel bad when you view an influencer on TikTok, or movie stars in videos, is due to social comparison, a concept first described in Chapter 2. Part of growing up is figuring out who you are and who you want to become. It's hard to sort these things out. You could ask your mom for help in figuring out who you are, but you know she's probably a bit biased because she's your mom. You could ask a friend how he views you, and he may tell you that you're "fun" and "talkative." He's probably biased, too. Most people who know you may offer only biased, positive feedback about who you are. People who don't really know you can't help with this dilemma. You're likely to look around to other people when trying to figure out who you are and who you want to be. You may decide that you want to have a haircut like Justin Bieber, and be as athletic as Alexander Robertson (a popular sports star in the UK) or Patrick Mahomes (a young American football player). Maybe you want to buy clothes like a popular guy at school, and you want to play football like your older brother.

In the process of thinking about your own identity, you look around at others and compare yourself with them. This is what social comparison is, and it's a valuable way to acquire information about yourself. Obviously, it matters a lot whom you compare yourself with. If you want to do well as a student, it may be a good idea to compare your study habits with your successful classmates. Comparing your practice habits with those of the team captain may help you become better at lacrosse. But you probably shouldn't compare yourself with celebrities. It's impossible to know what they really look like, because the images you see of them are edited. Celebrities are likely older than you, too, and have more money to spend on their appearance, clothes, and lifestyles. In many cases, they have personal trainers and personal chefs. They have expensive hair stylists, photographers, photo editors, and even people who help manage their images using social media (in other words, someone else posts for them on Instagram). In addition to issues of presentation, famous people and influencers are unlikely to be like you in a whole bunch of other ways.

MYTHS & MISBELIEFS

> **Social media use usually makes teenagers feel depressed and anxious.**

Adults have a lot of concerns about how social media affects young people, probably partially because they did not grow up with it and they don't tend to understand it as well as young people do. Not all adults' concerns are justified. In fact, there is some scientific evidence to suggest that social media can be a source of support for teens.

For example, a new study suggests that body-positive posts on social media (sometimes called #BoPo) may improve body satisfaction and overall mood. Another scientific study of Instagram use suggests that it has a more negative effect on body image when users spend more time in the public spaces of Instagram rather than connecting with people they know. Furthermore, although some research suggests that connecting with peers on social media may not always be a positive experience, connecting with family may be, perhaps because young people are more likely to compare themselves with other kids their age, but don't make these comparisons with their family. One way to make your use of social media a good experience is to be thoughtful about who you connect with, and to do your best to keep it positive.

(Note: If you're dealing with a serious health issue such as an **eating disorder** or depression, be sure that you don't rely on the internet or social media as your main source of support. You need a trained professional to help you. Also, be careful about the web pages that you visit; some offer inaccurate and even harmful information. We address these issues in more detail in Chapters 8 and 9.)

JUST BE YOU

There's a good chance that if someone has become famous, they weren't all that average to start with. This may sound depressing—it's not meant to—but you're probably average. Because that's the definition of average! "Average" is the way we describe what most people are like. There is nothing wrong with being average. In fact, if you think about it, there's something freeing about accepting that you're a normal, average person. You're special in many ways that the people who care about you appreciate, but you don't have to be exceptional, especially unique, or strive for fame. You can just be you.

Instead of growing up comparing yourself with an athlete or celebrity, maybe it makes sense to recognize that that's not who you are. Athletes and celebrities are a small minority of all people who are likely to be naturally gifted in particular ways. They may be unusually tall, or able to run really fast, or able to sing really well. Of course, it's possible that you have some of these qualities and talents, but you should appreciate that most people don't. And there is absolutely nothing wrong with that.

"LIKING," "FRIENDS," AND "FOLLOWERS"

Even if you do your best to ignore celebrity culture all together, you'll still be affected by the other people around you. In fact, with social media (for example, Instagram, Snapchat, TikTok) use on the rise, you may be virtually connected with a large social circle of people you don't really "know."

A recent study of more than 1,700 tweens and teens (8–18 years) in the USA showed that people in this age group spend more than an hour on social media every day; tweens spend about 5 hours on screens each day, while teens spend more than 7 hours each day. Most teens report liking social media, which makes sense—

otherwise you'd have to wonder why so many of them were using it! Where results from this study get a bit more interesting is in the questions about **self-presentation** (how teens try to present themselves on social media) and well-being. Many teens say that they present themselves how they actually are, but more say that they only share information and pictures that make them appear better than they may actually be. Sometimes people refer to this use of social media as posting the **highlight reel** of their lives, similar to how a preview for a movie may show some of the highlights from the movie.

Why is this issue of ideal self-presentation problematic? If teens only see each other's highlight reel—a filtered, edited collection of the best things they do—it's easy to compare themselves and feel like they don't look as nice and their lives aren't as exciting as others' are. This has the potential to make teens feel bad about themselves. Here again, social comparison is mostly to blame.

In spite of this, teens tend to report that social media is an important part of their social lives and it helps connect them to other people in ways that they like. This is not all teens' experience of social media, however. Teens who may be more **vulnerable** because they don't have as many friends, or because they're anxious or depressed, don't always view social media as a positive in their lives. For these teens, social media can be a painful reminder that they don't fit in, in a variety of ways, including how they look and the activity of their social lives. One of the important lessons is not to take social media too seriously.

EXPERT ADVICE

Professor Matthew Fuller-Tyszkiewicz, PhD, *Deakin University, Australia*

"We are all bombarded with images on TV, in movies, and on social media of muscle-bound men to compare ourselves to. It's deflating and de-motivating—I want to be healthy and in good shape, but are these masculine images **realistic**? At some point, we all need to decide whether it is realistic to aspire to look like these images. You might also consider whether lifting weights and regular, intense exercise are things you enjoy, and whether you even value trying to attain this physique. It is often healthier—physically and psychologically—to accept yourself as you are and not push yourself to be someone else."

VIDEO GAMES AND BIG "GUNS"

According to a 2019 report, tweens and teens spend more than an hour playing video games each day. However, there is a big gender difference, with boys playing significantly more video games than girls do. Almost half of boys spend more than 2 hours per day gaming. Video games tend to present players as avatars with exaggerated, idealized bodies and big "guns" (muscles—and possibly also big guns, but that's a topic for another book). The appearance of these avatars has been designed to appeal to boys, who are most likely to be gamers.

Although avatars may look how many boys (and men) would like to look, body image research suggests that these muscular avatars have a negative effect on boys' body image. For example, guys who were asked to play a wrestling game in one study reported feeling worse about their bodies after playing the game. Another study found that guys who played a video game with a super-muscular avatar experienced a decrease in their body satisfaction compared with guys who played the same video game with an avatar with a normal body build. Spending an hour (or more) every day with avatars with extreme muscles isn't harmless. This probably makes some sense to you. If you keep seeing guys who look a certain way, it isn't unreasonable for you to want to look like them—this is social comparison at work!

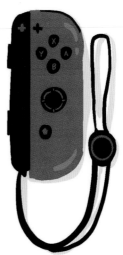

I don't want to stop using social media, but sometimes I wonder if I should. How do I know if it is worth it?

If people didn't like social media, or didn't feel that they got something out of using it, they probably wouldn't use it! It is valuable to think about whether or not there are more pros or cons to your social media use. Here are some of the factors you may want to consider:

PROS	CONS
Connecting with people	Distraction from other activities
Learning new things	Advertising can be annoying and misleading
Reading the news	Social comparison can be distressing
Entertainment	Unrealistic images and lifestyles are everywhere
Enjoyment	Possible negative impact on body image and /or mental health
A creative outlet	

Right now, your parents may have a lot of say in whether or not you use social media, and how much. This won't always be the case. You need to decide if you get a lot out of your social media use or if it isn't worth it to you. How do you want to be spending your time?

BECOME MEDIA LITERATE

One way to counter the negative effects of the **media** on your own body image is to become media literate. "**Literate**" usually means that you can read. When someone has **media literacy**, it means that person can "read" and understand what's going on in some form of media. In other words, they're critical of the media and try to decipher the intention of the media. This may be similar to what you're asked to do in school during reading comprehension exercises that involve reading a passage or story and deciphering what's going on in the text.

Why would you need to **analyze** and **evaluate** what's going on in the media you follow? As discussed in this chapter, the media isn't always honest in its **portrayal** of people and ideas. Social media may be the worst, as far as this is concerned. To be social media literate, think about people's **motivations** for posting, **techniques** they use to alter their pictures or posts, and how others may be presenting their best selves through their posts. How do you become media literate?

- First, every time you see an image in the media, remind yourself that the image isn't **realistic** and is probably edited and altered in a variety of ways. This is an important step in terms of maintaining a positive body image.
- Second, think about why the image is presented the way it is and pay attention to how it makes you feel.

- Third, stop comparing yourself with images you see and pay attention when images make you feel bad. Replace those bad feelings with positive feelings about yourself and focus on some of your strengths.
- Fourth, remember that the media is used to sell products and promote the idea that people have perfect lives. No one has a perfect life, and no one needs most of the products advertised.
- Fifth, remind yourself that you don't have to engage with any media. And you don't have to be active on all types of social media; you can ease into it, or not use some apps. You can turn off the television, delete an app from your phone, or stop yourself from responding to others' comments on social media. **You have control.**

Research suggests that being media literate can help protect your body image. Teens who are more critical of the media and think about the issues discussed above tend to have more positive feelings about their bodies. It's important that you don't view the media around you without trying to "read" it carefully.

FACE the media

To help you think about steps to take to keep different forms of media from having a negative effect on you, we have devised the acronym FACE (filter, avoid, careful of comparisons, evaluate). Take these steps to buffer yourself from the media:

- **Filter:** We aren't talking about filters in a photo editing tool or Snapchat. Body image researchers refer to something called protective filtering, which is essentially filtering out influences in your life that negatively affect your body image. If you notice that playing a certain video game or using a certain avatar while you play games makes you start to look sadly at your own biceps, then try to filter those games or avatars out of your life.

- **Avoid:** We all need media breaks (a point we'll return to in Chapter 5). Be sure you avoid your phone, tablet, computer, or however you view the media for some time every day. Eat dinner without texting your friends. Do homework without videos playing in the background. Sleep without the distraction of alerts coming from your devices.

- **Careful of comparisons:** As we've mentioned in this chapter, one of the ways that the media can be most harmful is by prompting us to compare ourselves with celebrities and other unrealistic portrayals of attractive people. Remember that these are not appropriate people to compare yourself with! The images that prompt social comparisons are usually of adults who have teams of people—fitness trainers, chefs, make-up artists, and professional photographers—who help make them look good. Most kids do not have teams of people working on their image, nor is this necessary.

- **Evaluate:** Not only do celebrities, athletes, and influencers have teams of people helping to make them look good, photographers and publicists are also editing and in some cases distorting their appearances to the point that these people don't even look like themselves. Why? In the places you see these people—Instagram, TikTok, or the internet—they are very likely trying to sell you a product or promote themselves and their "brand." Be skeptical and evaluate what you see. Why does the person look the way they do? How realistic is the image? What is for sale?

Some of my friends have begun **sexting** (exchanging **revealing** pictures) with their girlfriends. This makes me somewhat uncomfortable, but I'm not sure what (if anything) to say to them about this. It just seems like this may not be the best things to do.

Your instincts are probably correct that these aren't the safest activities for your friends to engage in. It's important to be proud of your body, but this doesn't necessarily mean that you should share it with the world (on social media), or even by sharing photos with a significant other.

One of the greatest risks is some other person seeing you partially clothed. Asking another person, like a girlfriend, to share a partially clothed picture puts them in a risky position as well. The chances are that no teenager wants the principal at their school, a future employer, or even their parents to see them partially clothed (in other words, partially naked). When a picture is shared online or using a smart phone, you have to consider the possibility that it will be shared with others and that it will end up archived online pretty much forever. Think about your future, and the future of people you care about!

In rare cases, teens have been charged with breaking child pornography laws when they've shared nude or sexually suggestive photos with others. This isn't what child pornography laws were designed for (they're meant to protect children and teens), but they were created before sexting existed. It's unlikely to happen, but because of these laws it's possible that sexting by those under 18 years of age can result in criminal charges.

If you ever feel pressured to send anyone a picture—or even just a message— that you aren't comfortable sending, stand up for yourself and say no. It is also important that you don't ask this of anyone else. If you really care about another person, you will not bully him or her into doing something that's embarrassing or uncomfortable, and you should expect that others will not bully you, either.

If you ever receive a message that you didn't want to receive, like a picture of someone else partially naked, delete it immediately. You don't want to have "pornography" stored on your phone or computer, as this also could possibly result in criminal charges.

If your friends aren't asking for your advice, or they aren't close friends, then you may want to keep your thoughts to yourself. Otherwise, perhaps you can share some of the information above and this will encourage them to change their behaviors.

MYTHS & MISBELIEFS

> You will lose contact with friends if you aren't on social media.

Many people—kids and adults alike—connect with others using social media. It's easy to feel like you'll miss out on these connections if you don't use social media or don't use a particular type of social media. You've probably heard this referred to as FOMO—fear of missing out.

It actually turns out that you may experience *less* FOMO if you spend *less time* on social media. A recent psychological study investigated college students' anxiety, depression, and concerns about being left out of activities. Half of the students who participated in the study used social media as they always had, and half were required to go on social media for a maximum of 30 minutes per day. The students who reduced their social media use to no more than 30 minutes per day for 3 weeks were less anxious and depressed and reported *less* FOMO. The scientists who conducted this study believe that when these young adults spent less time on social media, they engaged in fewer social comparisons. Fewer comparisons with others made them feel *better* about their own lives and less concerned about what others were doing!

If your friends use Snapchat to make plans and you delete the Snapchat app from your phone, you may feel worried that you won't be included in their plans. However, if your friends are truly good friends, they won't have a problem calling you or sending you a text instead when they are making plans. The science seems to suggest that fear of missing out isn't a great reason to use any particular type of social media.

THE CLOTHES MAKE THE MAN—OR DO THEY?

In 2020, Harry Styles, the heartthrob and musician (formerly of the band One Direction), created a stir by appearing on the cover of *Vogue* magazine wearing a dress. The article in the magazine also contained a series of photographs of him in a variety of dresses, skirts, and designer clothes. Styles wasn't the first musician to wear a dress; the rapper Young Thug has been called a fashion icon and wears mostly women's clothing, while musician David Bowie was frequently photographed in the 1970s wearing make-up, jumpsuits, and dresses. Why did people care what Styles was wearing? Do the clothes a man wears "make him"? Should you care what you wear?

As you become a teenager, it's totally normal for you to become concerned with your image and more interested in what you wear. After all, it's likely that for most of your childhood one of your parents bought your clothes and decided what you wore. It's time for you to take over those responsibilities. Your clothing choices may become an expression of your personality, identity, or preferences. For example, you may want to wear certain brands of clothing, or you may want to wear clothing items that say something on them—anything from your favorite sports team's logo to a favorite band's lyrics. You may enjoy shopping for clothes and selecting items to wear, or you may not. Some research suggests that boys and men feel like they should not care about their clothes—or how they look in general. However, this same research found that most do care and spend time picking out clothes and thinking about what looks good on them and what their friends wear.

You may also sometimes disagree with your parents or other adults about what you wear and other aspects of your appearance. Maybe you want to wear a sweatshirt and your parents insist that it is cold and you need to wear a jacket. Maybe you'd like to get your ears pierced or paint your fingernails, but your parents would rather that you didn't. Maybe you'd like to wear baseball hats all the time, but your parents want you to take off your hat in the house. One psychologist has suggested that when parents and their children disagree about things like clothing, it's rarely a disagreement only about clothing. Instead, children are pushing to make their own choices about something and parents are pushing back, not quite ready for their children to have that independence.

Parents may want you to look your age and also to look "respectable." They may be concerned about others judging you based on what you're wearing. Parents may also be thinking about your future and may not want your appearance to limit your choices; they may want you to look "responsible" so that you can earn your teachers' favorable opinion, gain work experience, participate in an internship, or be elected to a position on your student council.

Parents are also likely to want you to wear clothes that are comfortable and functional. In other words, your parents probably want you to wear clothes that do the job that clothes are supposed to do: cover your body comfortably. Men tend to value practicality and functionality in their clothes much more than women, but it's also fine if you are interested in fashion and less interested in comfort. Here's something interesting to think about, though, when it comes to clothing choices: If you feel uncomfortable with what you're wearing, you may spend time thinking about your appearance in a way that's distracting. It's most important that your clothes make you feel good psychologically, and that you are physically comfortable in them.

ACCEPT IT? OR FIX IT?

Clothes are not the only way to alter your appearance or make an impression on others. Maybe you're interested in getting your hair cut a particular way, letting it grow long, or even changing the color of it. Maybe you'd like to grow a beard, get a tattoo someday, or even permanently change some part of your appearance with surgery.

It's not uncommon for people to consider permanently changing some part of their appearance, whether it's getting a tattoo on their bicep or surgery to make their nose smaller. In fact, in 2019, a survey in the USA found that about 25% of adults have at least one tattoo; another survey found that 20% of British adults have tattoos. However, almost half of millennials (people born between 1982 and 2004) say they have a tattoo.

Some physical appearance changes are even more extreme. According to the most recent information from the **International Society for Aesthetic Plastic Surgery**, more than 11 million cosmetic surgical procedures were performed worldwide in 2019.

Although it used to be considered rebellious—or at least unusual—to permanently alter your appearance, it seems to be increasingly common. If you aren't happy with some aspect of your appearance, should you consider changing it—maybe even permanently?

There are a lot of things to keep in mind before you make any big decisions about permanently altering your looks. First, there are practical concerns. A lot of procedures are expensive. Tattoos may cost hundreds of dollars and cosmetic surgeries typically cost thousands. According to the **American Society of Plastic Surgeons**, the average cost of gynecomastia surgery (a breast reduction or reshaping for men, which is the most common procedure pursued among men worldwide in the search for "pecs") is more than $4,000. Most surgeries are safe, but there are always risks associated with surgery ranging from a painful recovery to not liking your changed appearance to much more serious consequences. There is always a slim chance that the medication used to put you to sleep during surgery (called anesthesia), or infections that are a result of surgery, could lead to serious or even deadly consequences.

Perhaps the most confusing issue when it comes to permanently altering your appearance is whether or not it's psychologically beneficial—will it actually make you feel better about yourself? Some body image researchers believe that an important part of developing a **positive body image** is accepting yourself and avoiding extreme practices such as cosmetic surgery. Furthermore, research suggests that changing your appearance doesn't completely change how people feel about themselves. In other words, if you get a nose job you might like your new nose better than your old nose, but you aren't likely to be happier overall. Your self-esteem is unlikely to be much higher. Once a few months (or years) have passed, you will probably be used to your new nose

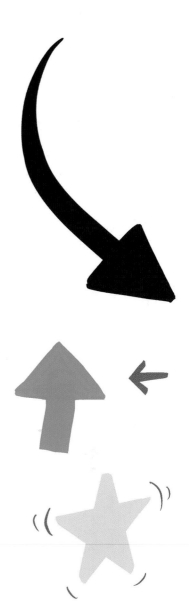

and not feel like it has changed your life in any significant way.

The advice that most body image experts give: is acceptance.

It's good advice to accept yourself as you are, but that doesn't mean that acceptance is always easy. As William reminds us below in his story, it is fairly normal to not always accept yourself or feel comfortable in your body.

One important thing to keep in mind is that you'll continue to change physically for most of your adolescence; remember everything discussed in Chapter 3? Even after your adolescence, you'll keep changing physically in ways that you can't predict now. If you ever do decide to make a permanent change to your appearance, wait until after you've finished puberty and you're well on your way to adulthood.

MY STORY

WILLIAM RYAN, 17 YEARS OLD

To be completely honest, I don't think that I have the most perfect-looking body, but at the same time I don't think it's awful either. I am on the skinny side. However, I think that I am more concerned with my health than the physical appearance of my body. If I developed a health issue, I would definitely feel more concerned about my body. Although I am sometimes self-conscious about the physical appearance of my body, I think that the health concerns would squash any other **insecurities** and matter much more to me.

I give some thought to what I eat, but not as much as other people that I know. I try to eat healthily, but that won't stop me from eating pizza or a cheesesteak on any given day. I think my eating habits are generally healthy so I don't feel bad when I eat unhealthy foods. Next summer, two of my close friends and I are planning to take a backpacking trip through the French and Swiss Alps after graduating high school. Planning for this trip has been the most I've ever thought about food in my life. We know we will need to find food that will keep us going, but doesn't cost too much money.

Continued ...

I would say that a combination of my friends and the media have been the most influential in the development of my thoughts and feelings about my body. Sometimes if I see my friends going on long runs or working out, it **motivates** me to try and do the same, but many of them are on competitive sports teams that require training. At the same time, some of my friends don't do any of those things, which reminds me that as long as you're healthy, you don't need to work out all the time. Additionally, I suppose that the media sends very mixed messages that affect how I feel about my body. On the one hand, I always see pictures and videos of people with perfect-looking bodies on TV, the internet, and social media, which often makes me think, "Wow, I wish that I looked like that." (Although I then always think to myself how much time and effort it would take to look like that... time that I sometimes find it hard to come by since I am always very busy). Nonetheless, I see many posts on social media about how you should be comfortable with your body, no matter what it looks like. I think that over the years I have become more comfortable with my body. I feel like the best way to put it is that I care, but I don't care that much. I don't want to feel terrible about my body, but it doesn't need to be perfect.

My advice for younger boys would be this: while all the time you might hear about how you should feel comfortable in your own skin, no matter what your body looks like, I have a different message. I think it is completely normal and very human to be insecure or uncomfortable with your body. If you're already comfortable with your body—that's great! But, if you aren't feeling good about yourself, there's nothing wrong with trying to take better care of yourself. I don't think it is necessary to eat certain foods or do certain types of exercise, but if you want to improve your health and how you feel about yourself, I see no reason not to.

Summing Up #BeYourOwnInfluencer

- ☑ Nearly all the pictures you see in the media are edited, and athletes, celebrities, and influencers have access to stylists and professional photographers. How you see them is not how they look "naturally"— just one of the reasons why it is important to become media literate.

- ☑ It's normal to compare yourself with others and want to look like people you admire, but try your best to appreciate your own unique qualities and avoid feeling insecure if you don't look like someone else.

- ☑ It may be tempting to try to change your appearance, whether by wearing certain clothes or even permanently altering your appearance, but always keep in mind that how you look is only one part of who you are, and no one looks "perfect" in real life.

Find out more

- If you're interested in reading more from Common Sense Media's reports about teens and social media use, check out their web pages: www.commonsensemedia.org/research/social-media-social-life-2018 and www.commonsensemedia.org/research/tweens-teens-tech-and-mental-health.

- James Potter has written a number of books specifically about media literacy that may be of interest, such as *7 Skills of Media Literacy* (2019). Publisher: SAGE Publications.

- For more information, check out the companion website to this book, www.TheBodyImageBookforBoys.com.

CHAPTER FIVE

MAKE YOUR BODY WORK FOR YOU

#FitnessJourney

"IF WE COULD GIVE EVERY INDIVIDUAL THE RIGHT AMOUNT OF NOURISHMENT AND EXERCISE, NOT TOO LITTLE AND NOT TOO MUCH, WE WOULD HAVE FOUND THE SAFEST WAY TO HEALTH."

Hippocrates, Greek physician, scientist

As you've probably noticed by now, a theme in this book is that it's important to take really good care of your body. One way to care for your body, and to keep it working for you, is to be physically active.

In this chapter you'll learn

○ about the benefits of physical activity for your body image and your health in general,

○ how to balance exercise and activity with other parts of a healthy life, and

○ techniques for establishing good health habits for physical activity or anything else that could benefit your health.

WHAT IS THE DIFFERENCE BETWEEN PHYSICAL ACTIVITY, EXERCISE, AND FITNESS?

Physical activity is any kind of movement of your body. Nearly anything that requires energy to do is physical activity: walking, running, playing basketball, swimming, mowing the lawn, and even cleaning your bedroom. Exercise is a particular type of physical activity that's usually more planned and intended to benefit your body. Playing on your school's basketball team is exercise: you do it regularly, it's structured, and you intend to be doing it. In contrast, you probably don't clean your room with the intention of strengthening your body, so it doesn't really count as exercise.

Often people talk about engaging in physical activity or exercise with the goal of being fit. Fitness is a broad term with more than one definition. People often talk about fitness in terms of getting in shape. What counts as fitness for one person may look very different for another person. The word fitness has become popular in recent years, as has the word fitspiration (aka "fitspo"). Fitspiration refers to images, **memes**, or ideas, usually shared on social media, that are supposed to inspire fitness. Unfortunately, there is some research to suggest that fitspiration isn't always inspiring. In fact, sometimes seeing images of fit people (usually muscular and impressive) just makes us feel bad about ourselves. Feeling bad about ourselves or feeling inferior to other people is rarely motivating. And it's not just fitspiration: much of the information about fitness that is available online lacks scientific support and may be harmful. Entire communities have developed online that promote unhealthy eating and exercise **behaviors**, so be sure you are only tuning into information online that is helpful and **evidence-based**.

MYTHS & MISBELIEFS

> Following fitness experts on Instagram will help motivate you to exercise regularly and get in shape.

Who doesn't like to feel inspired? Most people can use some inspiration (or "fitspiration" #Fitspo) to help them maintain good health habits, including regular physical activity. However, fitness experts on Instagram or other forms of social media may not be the best place to turn to for advice and inspiration. Usually, fitness "experts" and male celebrities and athletes are incredibly muscular, slim, and do little more than work on their fitness. That's their job—to look (and be) fit! In contrast, you most likely go to school, study, hang out with your friends, go to clubs, and do homework and chores—to name just a few of the activities that keep you, and people like you, busy every day. You don't have time to exercise all day. What this means is that fitness experts, celebrities, and professional athletes aren't usually a good source of comparison (or inspiration) because you have a much busier life.

As we learned earlier, psychologists call mental comparisons of ourselves with others social comparison. Upward social comparison is when we're comparing ourselves with others who are "above" us, or more accomplished than us. The result is that we usually feel bad about ourselves. In fact, in one recent study, exposure to fitspiration images on social media was linked to higher rates of eating-disorder symptoms. Participants not only felt bad about themselves after viewing what were intended to be inspirational images, but they may have been more likely to adopt unhealthy eating habits as well. In another study, fitspiration images affected how guys felt about their muscles—and it didn't make them feel good. Turns out, fitspiration is usually not all that inspirational.

EXPERT ADVICE

Cody Miller, *Olympic swimmer, USA*

"I've been able to meet all sorts of people—celebrities, models, athletes—the 'perfect' people. But I've learned that everyone has something about themselves that they don't like. Everyone has insecurities, and the sooner you accept that there is no 'perfect,' the sooner you can move past your insecurities. Shame only lives in the darkness. Confronting your insecurities allows your confidence to grow."

HOW MUCH ACTIVITY IS IDEAL?

Most kinds of movement are good for you. Obsessing about how much you exercise is usually not. The US Department of Health and Human Services recommends that kids aged 6–17 years engage in 1 hour of physical activity a day. That may sound like a lot, but remember that physical activity can include all sorts of things. If you walk to school, or even walk around while you're at school, you may easily find yourself active for 30 minutes most days.

Some of this activity is likely to be aerobic. If you're working up a sweat and breathing heavily, either because you ran up some stairs at school or because you've gone for a jog at home, then this is aerobic activity. Even a fast-paced walk is aerobic activity. It's valuable to also take part in physical activity that's good for your muscles and bones. This can include stretching and working on flexibility, practicing yoga, doing push-ups or sit-ups, and even lifting weights as you get older. Not everyone finds physical activities that they enjoy early in life, as Dawson's story suggests.

DAWSON JONES, 16 YEARS OLD

How I feel about my body varies a lot by the day. Some days, I will wake up and be very happy with the way I look, while other days I am not happy with my body at all. Most days I fall somewhere in between.

I do exercise, although for a lot of my life I struggled to find something that I enjoyed and that I was somewhat good at. In the past, I have played baseball, tennis, and soccer independently of school, and in gym classes at school I have played other team sports. I never enjoyed any team sports and I was never any good at them. In middle school, I was a part of the cross-country team and track, but similar to other sports, despite my training, I never enjoyed them at all! I had a difficult time keeping up with anyone else on the team and I consistently finished last in competitions and races. In my sophomore year of high school, I joined a weightlifting class that I did not hate and I started to see improvements in my fitness, but this was brought to an abrupt end by the pandemic in the spring of 2020 and the closing of schools.

Over the last few months, I have discovered that I have a passion for mountain biking, and luckily, I have a system of fairly challenging uphill and

Continued ...

downhill trails only a few minutes from my house.
I live right at the foothills of the mountains
in Colorado where I have begun biking 5-10 miles
at least a few days per week. I am excited to
pursue this interest and join the mountain biking
team at my school and enter in various races and
competitions.

As I have gotten older, I have become a lot more
self-conscious about the way I look, to the
point where I swim in a shirt and I am extremely
uncomfortable and embarrassed in any situation
where I might have to take it off. I cannot think
of a specific moment where my perceptions about my
body changed, but it seems that my friends have no
problem taking their shirts off at the pool, and I
wish that I felt the way they seem to about this.

My advice to younger boys is to know that every
person looks different, and that there is not just
one definition of what people are supposed to look
like, and to accept yourself for who you are. At
least, that is what I am trying to do!

WHAT ARE THE BENEFITS OF PHYSICAL ACTIVITY?

Why try to be regularly active? There is a great deal of scientific research to suggest that regular physical activity is good for both your psychological and physical health. Kids who are physically active tend to be more fit and have stronger bones and muscles. In fact, almost every part of your body benefits from physical activity: your heart, lungs, digestive system, immune system (which fights infection), even the genes in your cells, seem to gain protection from physical activity. Being physically active is also associated with better mental health and lower rates of depression. Even light activity—a couple of hours per week—has been linked with better mental health as kids get older. Being physically active may even be good for your brain and your ability to learn.

Perhaps most important, though, is that if you are regularly active you are more likely to develop an appreciation for how good you feel when you move your body. You're more likely to develop good habits you stick with as you get older. If you develop a love for swimming when you're young, you're more likely to swim as a form of exercise when you're an adult. We all become more vulnerable to health problems as we get older, including heart disease, type 2 diabetes, and cancer. Being active can help prevent some of these health problems and may even help us live longer lives.

FINDING WHAT YOU LOVE

Some of you reading this book will feel like you're not sure how to work physical activity into your life because you just don't like sports, or don't feel like you're very good at any of them. Not all of us are good at sports, and although it is possible to get better at some sports by practicing, there is a bit of natural talent (or lack of talent) that determines athletic performance. If you feel like you don't have natural talent, then playing some sports may just make you feel stressed out or self-conscious.

Fortunately, being physically active doesn't mean that you have to play a sport. There are a lot of ways to get yourself moving. Here are some ideas, in alphabetical order: acrobatics, badminton, cycling, dance, exercise classes, fencing, gymnastics, horseback riding, ice skating, jumping rope, kickboxing, line dancing, martial arts, netball, Oztag (a type of rugby), Pilates, quoits, rock climbing, stretching, tai chi, ultimate Frisbee, volleyball, walking, Xtreme paintball, yoga, and Zumba.

MYTHS &
MISBELIEFS

> It's important to stretch before you do any vigorous exercise.

First, it is important to define what is meant by stretching. There are generally two types of stretches: static and dynamic. A *static* stretch refers to just holding a position that "pulls" at a muscle or stretches it, such as a lunge position to stretch your quadriceps (the top, front leg muscle). A *dynamic* stretch refers to moving in a way that stretches or loosens up muscles without just holding a position. So, instead of a lunge position, you could do wide, slow jumping jacks to stretch out your leg muscles. Athletes usually use dynamic stretching and view it as superior, but there is very little research examining how much either form of stretching prepares the body for exercise and peak performance.

Some research suggests that athletes who use static stretching, dynamic stretching, or who don't do any stretching at all seem equally prepared for exercise. This is determined through the use of controlled experiments in exercise laboratories.

In contrast, warming up, which tends to include some jogging and movement that is similar to the exercise or sport the individual is about to engage in, has been shown to help prevent injuries. One such warm-up program, the FIFA 11+, has been tested among thousands of soccer players including both kids and adults. Those who used the warm-up program experienced fewer knee, ankle, hip, and groin injuries. If you play hockey, for example, you'll want to learn warm-ups that are relevant to the muscles worked when you play. Your coach will likely have suggestions for you, and you should pay attention to what works best for you.

The **bottom line** is that stretching particular muscles is not important to athletic performance or to injury prevention, but warming up muscles is probably a good idea.

ARJUN MUHAMMAD, 22 YEARS OLD

I feel okay-ish about my body. If I was to rate my body, I would give it a 7.5/10. The reason why I say so is because I like to look at my body in two ways. One is the outer surface—the one that people see. I am healthy and I eat healthy food, but I am not toned. I am working out to have a better body every day, but I am not fully satisfied with my outer looks. The second way I look at my body is on the inside. I eat healthily, I feel healthy, and I take very good care of my body. I do frequent skin care to make sure that I am clean as well.

Growing up, I always played soccer, so eating the right food with proper nutrients was essential. I have always loved the sport, and there was nothing more that I looked forward to than playing soccer. My mother always made sure that we were not eating too much junk food and were eating **nutritious** food. My family also has a history of diabetes, so we make sure our diet is not further worsening the situation. My mother, her parents, and my father's parents are diabetic, so my mother was extra cautious about making sure I ate healthy options. Even when I am by myself, I try to avoid sugar as much as possible and try to eat healthy options so I can take care of my body and be fit. Being healthy is important to me and makes me feel good about myself.

My best friend, Andrew, has played a big role in the development of my thoughts and feelings about my body. He is one person who has always motivated me because he is very disciplined. He wakes up every morning at 5 a.m. to run and then go work out in the gym. He's encouraged me to go to the gym with him, and when we hang out together, we are careful to eat healthy food, too.

Continued ...

My biggest advice for younger boys is to just let your body grow naturally. I feel like the average age for boys to start working out in the gym is getting younger and younger by the day. I see 13-year-old kids' videos on Instagram that show them lifting weights in the gym. It's great for boys to be active and play sports, but it's unhealthy to be obsessive. Boys should be attempting to stay fit not because they want their body to look good in photos, as today's social media shows, but to feel better about themselves. It's also important for boys (and all people) to realize that working out is not the only way to feel good about yourself; there are other ways, too. At the end of the day, a good body won't get you into a good college or get you a job, but a good personality and a good education will!

Many people try a lot of different activities out before they find something they love. At different stages in your life, you may try different activities. Right now, being on your school's football team or swim team may be a lot of fun and good exercise, but as you get older you may find yourself riding a bike to school or walking your dog to get exercise.

It's valuable to think creatively when it comes to ways to move your body. Maybe you'll find that you love DIY projects around the house or enjoy playing golf with a friend. You don't have to be competitive (or even social) to be physically active, and there are an endless number of options. Be creative in thinking about ways to keep your body fit and make it work for you.

I know that exercise is good for you, but what about sports like American football and soccer that have been getting a bad rap because athletes are at risk of concussion? Are head injuries and concussions that serious or likely to occur?

American football and soccer (aka football in countries outside the USA) are extremely popular sports. Many kids around the world grow up watching and playing these sports, but playing them is not without risk, and many parents are beginning to limit their children's playing as a result.

Perhaps the most concerning risk associated with playing contact sports like football and soccer is concussion, which is a type of traumatic brain injury. When a player experiences a blow to the head, or a blow to the body (it does not need to be a direct head hit) that causes the head to jolt and move back and forth, damage to the brain can result. These injuries are not usually fatal, but they can be serious.

Chronic traumatic encephalopathy (CTE) is a form of brain damage that has been diagnosed in many former professional football and hockey players. CTE is thought to be caused by many concussions. It can be quite serious and has been found to contribute to memory loss, depression, and dementia.

It is difficult to know how often CTE occurs in athletes, particularly among those who do not become professionals. Part of the challenge is that CTE can only be diagnosed after people die. This usually means that families of professional athletes who have died and exhibited symptoms of CTE—memory loss, depression, dementia—have to ask doctors to examine the athletes' brains. Among deceased professional US football players whose bodies were made available to doctors for inspection of their brains, recent research published

Continued ...

in the *Journal of the American Medical Association* suggests that nearly all showed signs of CTE. Remember, though, that doctors only look at the brains of people whose families suspected they had suffered from CTE. We don't know how common CTE is in former professional football players who haven't yet died, or among those who have died, but whose families did not ask for their brains to be examined. Playing soccer as a kid and playing professional football are very different experiences, but it is important to take good care of yourself if you experience a head injury. The box below describes signs and symptoms of a concussion that you should be aware of if you play a contact sport. Look out for these and don't return to playing too soon if you experience a concussion. A repeat injury before you're fully healed can be extremely dangerous and even life-threatening.

Signs and symptoms of concussion	Treatment of concussion
• Confusion • Inability to remember events prior to the injury • Feeling stunned • Loss of consciousness • Behavior or personality changes • Headache or pressure in the head • Nausea or vomiting • Dizziness • Blurred vision • Sensitivity to light or noise • Lack of concentration • Sluggishness • Depression • Not feeling normal or "right"	• See a doctor • Do not play sports or engage in physical activity until a doctor approves your return • Rest more than usual • Avoid lights (such as television or your phone) and sounds that bother you or keep you from resting • Be sure that your parents, coaches, and healthcare providers communicate about your injury, treatment, and when you can resume being active

WHY BEING ACTIVE CAN MAKE YOU FEEL GOOD ABOUT YOUR BODY

There are so many benefits to being regularly active—everything from learning new skills to having fun with friends can be valuable. And there is evidence that physical activity can increase positive feelings about your body.

You may recall the discussion of body functionality from Chapter 2. Basically, the idea is that focusing on how our bodies work or function is an important part of nurturing a positive body image. Recent body image research suggests that playing sports *decreases* negative feelings boys may have about their bodies and *increases* positive feelings they have about them. Feeling good about your body can also increase participation in sports. There may be a cycle that occurs for some people, with physical activity improving their body image, which in turn leads them to participate in more physical activity.

This doesn't mean that you need to play sports or to be an athlete to reap the rewards of physical activity. Remember, any sort of movement counts as physical activity! And any movement that you do regularly can help you think more about the many amazing things that your body can *do*, which is way more valuable than how your body looks.

ESTABLISHING GOOD HABITS

Maybe the idea of participating in more physical activity is growing on you. How do you get in the habit of being more active? It's often difficult for people to change their habits, but there are some evidence-based practices that will help.

First of all, don't aim too high. That may sound sort of pessimistic, but it's easy to set an unreasonable fitness goal and then find it impossible and give up all together. Set a small goal that you know that you can achieve. Maybe your goal is to walk your dog for 10 minutes each day, or join a karate class with a friend each week. Do something that will be fairly easy to accomplish. Once you do this new activity for a few weeks, consider adding another change. Maybe walk your dog for 15 minutes per day, or run with your dog instead of walking. Maybe add in a second karate class per week, or shoot some hoops with your friend after school. When you set small, achievable goals and you're successful, that success will **motivate** you to do more. If it doesn't, then reconsider your goals. Maybe you don't really like karate. Maybe you'd rather go to a gym instead of walking your dog.

Another important consideration if you're trying to add physical activity to your regular routine is that you may have to take something else out of your regular routine. There are only so many hours in the day. If your schedule is already packed full, you may need to drop something to add physical activity. Be sure you don't drop other valuable activities like spending enough time on your homework, or getting enough sleep. If you spend a lot of time playing video games or watching videos, it may make sense to do some sort of physical activity instead.

Telling people about your goals and asking for help in achieving them can also be helpful. Scientists call this a **commitment strategy**. We tend to be more likely to stick with a goal if other people know about it. We don't want to feel embarrassed if others realize we didn't stick with our goal. It can also be valuable to ask people for help in meeting our goals. Maybe you'd like a parent or a friend to remind you of your activity goals, or maybe you want a friend to exercise with you. Either way, it can be useful to have supportive people in your life helping you achieve any of the goals that you have.

Finally, be patient with yourself and don't give up. If you don't follow through with whatever activity goal you've set for yourself, don't throw in the towel forever. Maybe your life feels too busy right now, but once summer rolls around, you'll have more time and you can work on setting new activity goals. Once you establish a habit for 2–3 months, it tends to stick, but you have to keep at it before the sticking happens. People tend to be creatures of habit, and changing those habits isn't easy. Be patient with yourself if you don't meet your goals the first time you try. Most people have to try more than once to change any habit.

TAKE IT OUTSIDE

One thing that may help you stick to a physical activity regimen is to exercise outside. A number of scientific studies have examined how people feel about exercise that's done outside versus inside. Usually, participants in this research are asked to do something like go for a walk outside or walk on a treadmill inside. Not only do people tend to say that they like walking outside more, but they even report feeling less tense and less depressed after a walk outside. The same doesn't seem to be true of walking on a treadmill. People seem to find outdoor physical activity easier, too. Walking on a treadmill is a good way to get some exercise, but if you don't enjoy it that much, it'll be hard to stick with it. The trick to being regularly active is to find something that you like enough to keep doing it.

If being outside might make physical activity more pleasurable, what else can you do outside? In addition to walking, running and hiking are great outdoor activities. Nearly any sport can be played outside. Biking, football, and basketball are all good outdoor activities. In the summer, you may want to swim or surf (depending on where you live), and in the winter, you may want to ski or snowboard (again, depending on where you live). However, if the weather or other circumstances don't allow you to exercise outdoors, still try to find ways to move indoors. In research comparing people's moods after they sit around indoors versus exercise indoors, active folks were in better moods and felt more relaxed than the people who sat around, even if they were allowed to play on a computer while they sat. So even though you may think that you prefer to spend your free time playing video games or watching television shows, science suggests that you'll feel better if you get outside and move. (See more about screen time later in this chapter.)

Is it possible to be too young to work out? Are there types of physical activity that are good for younger guys compared with older guys?

In general, physical activity is good for both your mental and physical health, provided you don't have any health problems that would keep it from being safe. Don't try to run if you've sprained your ankle, or throw a ball if you've broken your arm. Furthermore, if you have a heart condition or other health concern, be sure to talk with your doctor and parents about what is safe for you.

The safest type of physical activity for any age is probably walking, although more strenuous physical activity has benefits if you are able. The Mayo Clinic (a prestigious medical center in the USA) suggests that strength training is safe during childhood. Push-ups, sit-ups, and exercises that use the body's own weight for resistance are the safest until a teen's bones are fully grown. It's not possible to be sure when your bones are done growing, so be careful in the strength exercises you participate in before your late teens. Many doctors advise against trying to build muscle by lifting heavy weights until the end of puberty.

CAN YOU EXERCISE TOO MUCH?

Watching professional athletes and people who enjoy being active can be so inspiring. It can make you want to devote more of your time and energy to achieving your own fitness potential. Physical activity is incredibly good for your body and your mind, but, as with anything, there can be too much of a good thing.

Some research suggests that participating in regular, vigorous exercise such as jogging can add 5–6 years on to your lifespan. But if you want to live a long time, it may be best to be more moderate in your approach to exercise (for example, not exercising every day). It's safe to conclude that exercise is nearly always good for you physically. However, it's important to listen to your body. If you're tired all the time, really hungry from exercising, or not enjoying exercising anymore, then you're probably overdoing it.

I've heard a lot about high-intensity interval training (HIIT) recently. What is it, and is it a good idea?

High-intensity interval training (HIIT) has received a lot of attention in recent years, probably because people like the idea of training hard ("high intensity") for short periods of time. Usually, HIIT workouts involve alternating between nearly all-out exertion (for example, running as fast as you can) and lower exertion (for example, jogging) for intervals of a minute or so each. Sometimes the high-intensity parts of the workout last for 30 seconds and the lower-intensity parts last for a few minutes; there are no set rules, really. The idea is to push yourself for short periods of time, and the total length of the workout is often under 30 minutes.

There is some evidence that HIIT workouts can be a good way to increase your fitness, and are at least as good as longer workouts at a mid-level of exertion (for example, running at a medium pace for you). Some fitness experts have suggested that HIIT workouts burn more fat than regular workouts, but a recent review of the scientific research suggests that is not always the case. If you enjoy interval training, then work it into your exercise routine. But if you don't, then don't worry about it. Any kind of physical activity is usually good for you.

It's also possible that your body will respond in a very serious manner to physical overexertion. For example, in extremely rare cases of people who exercise for long periods of time every day for months, muscles can break down and kidney damage can occur (this is called rhabdomyolysis). The lesson is: be active, but use common sense.

It also seems pretty clear that too much exercise can have a negative effect on your mental health, especially if exercising feels like an obligation and not like something that you enjoy. Psychologists sometimes refer to exercise that feels necessary, especially more than once per day, as compulsive exercise. It has become trendy for men to compulsively exercise and focus on weightlifting in an attempt to build muscle. This is sometimes referred to as bulking (eating excessively while lifting heavy weights), cutting (reducing body fat while maintaining muscle), and shredding (working on muscle definition or getting ripped). As we describe in the Q & A on the next page, although lifting heavy weights *may* help you build muscle, most of the "plans" that you see for building muscle online or on Instagram are not developed by scientists with the education and training to offer good advice. Avoid these sorts of plans and any recommendations that seem extreme. Extreme approaches to exercise can absolutely do more harm than good for your health.

If you feel like you're scheduling your day around exercise, worrying about how much you exercise, feeling guilty if you don't exercise, not eating unless you exercise a certain amount, or eating more to support your exercise habit, you may be a compulsive exerciser. Compulsive exercise can be dangerous for your mental health and you should talk to someone—a parent, school counselor, or therapist—if you think this describes you. Being regularly physically active can be great, but if you push yourself all the time and are not enjoying your activity, it's time to step back and rethink things.

PAUL BRIAN, 16 YEARS OLD

I believe I've come a long way from where I was years ago. I stopped doing sports for a while and I let myself go. I got out of shape and I had a lot of unhealthy habits. Then, I discovered ultimate Frisbee, and it allowed me to run around. With near-daily practices with my ultimate team, I have slimmed down and feel comfortable about my general shape.

I play ultimate Frisbee at an advanced level and I run to keep myself quick on the field. Over the winter, I work out one to two times per week to stay in condition, and I occasionally run 5 kilometers. I play ultimate Frisbee for fun, and I run and work out to better my playing.

I don't remember in much detail how I used to feel at the pool, but I remember that I would try to get in as soon as possible to avoid my stomach being in sight of others. Early on when I played ultimate Frisbee, I would feel uncomfortable at pick-up games because you would wear either a light or dark shirt, and if I had to change, I would rush taking off and putting on my shirt. I think any moment where my shirt was off in public just caused me to feel embarrassed and uncomfortable.

I feel like I've shifted from being self-conscious to wanting to take good care of myself. I try to eat healthily and to not eat too much before physical activity like running so I don't feel terrible. I am constantly reminded by my parents to stop eating whatever I lay my eyes on, which keeps me from making too many unhealthy choices. I do still like to enjoy junk foods sometimes and I don't feel guilty about that.

If I had to tell my younger self one thing about growing up, I would let him know that it will take time to feel comfortable in your body, but it will happen.

I've grown taller in the last year, but I feel like I'm scrawny and don't have the body I wish I did. What is the best way to build muscle?

There is probably no question we hear more from boys and young men than this one. Unfortunately, boys and men tend to equate muscles with attractiveness and manliness. It is not your fault if you think this; you have learned this from a society that views men's muscles as attractive.

Regular exercise is physically and psychologically valuable and can lead to changes in the appearance of your body. It is very likely that you will acquire some muscle mass if you are regularly active. However, while changing your body shape and muscularity is more possible than changing your height (which is almost completely down to your genes), it can still be very difficult to go from lean and slender to muscular.

A recent study (which examined monkeys, but scientists think that humans' bodies function similarly) suggests that building muscle is incredibly complex. It starts with changes in our nervous system, not our muscles. Some people, especially women and boys before puberty, often don't build much muscle at all, even though they will get stronger. Muscles "grow" not just because of weightlifting, but because of changes in nerve communication between our brains and bodies.

The **bottom line** is that changing the appearance of your body may require you to spend a lot more time being active and lifting weights than you have to devote to these activities. It's important to be physically active, but also important to remember that how you feel is more important than how you look.

AND MAKE SURE YOU REST, TOO

It's important to your health that you keep your body moving, but it's equally important that you make sure your body gets enough rest. More than half of all middle schoolers and high schoolers (ages 11–18 years, approximately) in the USA don't get enough sleep. How much sleep do you get most nights? Think about what time you usually get into bed, when you usually fall asleep, and when you usually wake up. Are you sleeping at least 8 or 9 hours each night?

The Centers for Disease Control and Prevention (CDC) recommends that 6–12-year-olds need 9–12 hours of sleep each night, and 13–18-year-olds need 8–10 hours of sleep each night. Sleep is related to pretty much every aspect of your health and well-being. Although the relationship between sleep and different sorts of diseases is complicated, not getting enough sleep may place you at risk for type 2 diabetes, heart disease, weight gain, and even depression. At the very least, not sleeping enough is a way to feel miserable, tired, and cranky the next day. Making sure you get enough sleep is one thing you can do to take care of yourself and protect your mental and physical health.

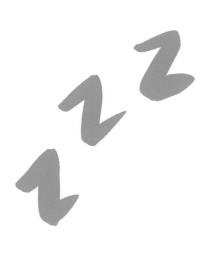

If you aren't sure you're getting enough sleep, or you want to try to get more sleep (you can't sleep too much!), here are some things you might want to try:

- Go to bed at the same time each night and wake up at the same time.
- Make sure your bed is comfortable to you.
- Make sure the room you sleep in is a comfortable temperature, not too hot or too cold.
- Don't eat a big meal too close to bedtime.
- Be careful not to drink anything with caffeine (such as soda or tea) in the afternoon or evening.
- Keep electronic devices out of your bedroom.
- Don't do other things in bed where you sleep. Don't study, watch television, or eat on your bed.

WHAT IF YOU CAN'T FALL ASLEEP?

The thing that keeps people from sleeping more than anything else is... worrying about not being able to fall asleep!

If the above tips are not helpful and you are not getting enough sleep, it may be that you are experiencing anxiety, depression, or a sleep disorder. We'll talk more about anxiety and depression in Chapter 9, but there are plenty of steps you can take to improve your sleep. You may want to try some

relaxation exercises or listen to relaxing music when you go to sleep. Sleeping well has a lot to do with forming good sleep habits and getting used to enjoying sleep, as opposed to feeling anxious in bed at night.

It isn't uncommon for people to think about their days and even to worry a bit when they lie in bed at night. If you find yourself worrying a lot, you may want to talk with a parent or other adult that you feel comfortable talking to, like a grandparent, an older sibling, or a counselor at your school. Sometimes just talking about what's on your mind can help a lot. Often, other people can help you understand that some of the things you're worried about are unlikely to happen, or unlikely to matter very much in the grand scheme of things. This isn't to say that your worries are anything to be embarrassed about, just that getting other people's perspective can be valuable.

If talking with someone about your worries and adopting healthy sleep habits don't do the trick, then you may want to talk with a doctor. It's possible that you have a sleep disorder (although a true sleep disorder is fairly rare before adulthood, affecting just 4% of children, according to the Association of American Family Physicians). Sleep is really crucial to your overall health, so be sure to get the help you need to ensure you sleep well and enough.

DON'T SACRIFICE SLEEP FOR THE SCREEN

If you're like a lot of kids these days, you have a parent who talks about screen time more than you'd like. Your parent is probably in line with what the American Academy of Pediatrics (AAP; the biggest organization of doctors that focus on kids' health in the USA) recommends for kids' screen time, or as they put it, a "healthy media diet." They suggest that parents put limits on screen time and make sure their kids don't let screens interfere with sleep, physical activity, and health in general. They also advise parents to make sure that kids experience media-free times with their families, such as dinnertime. The AAP recommends that families sit down and talk about their media use and create a plan together.

Why is this in the chapter on physical activity? You've probably heard adults grumble that when they were kids they ran around outside and didn't spend all their time using a phone or a tablet. You've probably also heard that kids are more likely to weigh more

EXPERT ADVICE

Chris Mosier, *duathlete, triathlete, and first transgender athlete to make it on to the US National Team in the gender in which they identify*

"As an athlete, my body is my tool and my vehicle for achieving my dreams. There's no one right way to have a body, or to be an athlete, or to be a transgender person. Once we stop worrying about what others will think of us or say about us, the whole entire world opens up."

than in past generations. Those two things are linked: more screen time tends to mean less physical activity, which may lead to weight gain. It's important to find some sort of balance. Watching television or videos and playing video games can be entertaining, but taking good care of your body means making it move around most days.

IT'S NEVER TOO LATE

Maybe you aren't particularly interested in being more physically active than you already are, or you just don't have the time, with school and other activities you're involved in. This is OK. We're all works in progress and we have the potential to become better in the future, whether that means becoming more knowledgeable about a particular topic, more involved in a certain hobby, or more engaged in physical activity.

Being a kid means juggling school, relationships with family and friends, and other extracurricular activities. If you don't want to, or just can't find the time to do *one more* activity or responsibility right now, this isn't a reason to feel guilty. It can be tough to be a kid!

As you get older, you're likely to find more occasions and opportunities to engage in physical activity of all types. So even if you don't get into a particular form of exercise now, this doesn't mean that you won't when you're older. Physical activity will benefit your mind and body, even if you don't make it a habit until you're an adult. We are all on our own fitness journeys and should do our best to make physical activity a healthy part of our lives.

Summing Up #FitnessJourney

- ☑ Being regularly physically active is an important part of taking care of your body and nurturing a positive body image.

- ☑ Physical activity can improve not just how you feel about yourself, but your mental and physical health as well. Being regularly active can even help you live a longer life.

- ☑ Don't sacrifice sleep to exercise, and be careful not to let screen time take the place of sleep or physical activity. It's important to find some balance so you do things you enjoy (watching TV), things you have to do (homework), and things that are important for your health (physical activity and sleep). It can be difficult to achieve this balance, so be sure to ask friends or family for help establishing good habits.

Find out more

- The Centers for Disease Control and Prevention's website includes information about physical activity and sleep habits: www.cdc.gov/physicalactivity/index.html and www.cdc.gov/sleep/index.html.

- The Centers for Disease Control and Prevention's website also includes information about concussion: www.cdc.gov/headsup/pdfs/youthsports/parents_eng.pdf

- The American Academy of Pediatrics has an online worksheet that families can use to discuss the important issues around balancing media time: www.healthychildren.org/English/media/Pages/default.aspx.

- For more scholarly articles and web pages with information about physical activity see the companion website for this book: www.theBodyImageBookforBoys.com.

CHAPTER SIX

FUEL YOUR BODY

#Nutrition101

"ASK NOT WHAT YOU CAN DO FOR YOUR COUNTRY. ASK WHAT'S FOR LUNCH."

Orson Welles, American actor, writer, and director

What and how much you eat affects your health and body image. Taking care of our bodies means feeding them well.

In this chapter you'll learn

○ why it's important to eat *intuitively* and select nutritious foods to eat—most of the time,

○ basic nutritional information about different kinds of food: fats, carbs, protein, sugar, salt, fiber, fruits and vegetables, and

○ the information you need to think about food as **nourishment** for your body and eating as contributing to a positive body image.

THE "HOW MUCH" OF EATING

Once you begin puberty, you may notice that on some days you feel really hungry, like a bottomless pit, and other days you're hardly hungry at all. This is totally normal. As you go through puberty, you'll grow a lot (see Chapter 3 for more information about puberty), and this growth is likely to make you hungry and lead you to eat. You'll need to eat more during puberty than you did before, but unfortunately there's no simple way to figure out how much to eat on any given day. One approach to figuring out how much to eat is to pay attention to the signals your body gives you. You can guide your eating by attending to cues like how full your stomach feels, and how much hunger you experience. This is called **intuitive eating**.

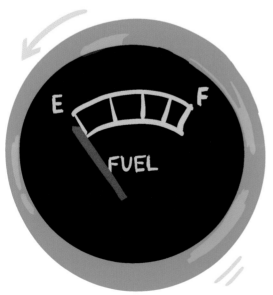

We all learn food "rules" from our culture, like the rules to eat three meals a day, or not to eat before swimming or sleeping. If you're eating intuitively, you ignore most (if not all) of these rules. This doesn't necessarily mean that you

just eat whatever you want whenever you feel like it. I'm sure you already know that doughnuts every day for breakfast, a burger and fries for every lunch, and spaghetti and meatballs for each dinner wouldn't be the healthiest way to eat all the time. Intuitive eating is *thoughtful* eating. When you feel hungry, think "what would taste good right now?" *and* "what would be good for me right now?" Sometimes the answer may be ice cream, but it probably shouldn't be ice cream all the time. The goal of intuitive eating is to pay attention to when your body signals hunger *and* when your body feels full of food.

We aren't always good at knowing the amount of food we need to eat. Scientific evidence supports the popular saying that your brain needs time for your stomach to know it's full. When you eat, the food travels to your stomach, which gradually expands as the food accumulates. Your stomach has to send that information to your brain, and that can take around 20 minutes. This is why after eating a big dinner you may not realize that you're full until you feel uncomfortable 20–30 minutes later. You didn't feel that full while you were eating your fourth slice of pizza, but once your brain caught up with what was going on, you started to realize that you'd feel better if you unbuttoned that top button on your jeans.

Paying attention to your body and your eating habits is really important. You want to feel nourished by food, to enjoy eating, and to create good habits that you'll stick with as you become an adult.

THE "WHAT" OF EATING

What should you eat? The simple answer to this question is: anything and nearly everything—in moderation. Some foods are much better for your body than others, but this doesn't mean that you need to completely avoid less nutritious options. Foods that are not particularly nutritious—ice cream,

EXPERT ADVICE

Virginia Sole-Smith, journalist and author of *The Eating Instinct*, USA

"For a long time, I thought my job as a health and **nutrition** journalist was to tell people how to eat. But then I noticed something: the 'rules'—and the science behind them—kept changing. Like, I bet if you ask your parents, they grew up thinking fat was bad. Now, everyone freaks out about sugar, or other ingredients. We're also even more inundated with these rules, thanks to social media. Pretty much anyone can call themselves a health influencer and claim they know how you should eat. But nobody else can tell how hungry or full you are. Nobody else should be in charge of whether you eat some chips because you have a ton of studying to do and the crunching helps you focus. We eat for a million different reasons, all of them valid. Now I know that nutrition can be useful information, but it's just one piece of the puzzle. The best way to have a healthy relationship with food is to start by trusting your body."

crackers, and candy—usually taste good! The next chapter will discuss in more detail why it can actually be valuable to eat some of these foods even though they aren't super nutritious. You don't need to totally give up any food that you enjoy, but you do want to be sure that you're eating enough foods that are nutritionally valuable so you continue to grow and protect your health.

How exactly is the **nutritional value** of food measured? There are a variety of ways that foods can be categorized. What we mean by nutritional value is that foods provide various types of **nutrition** through proteins, carbohydrates, fats, vitamins, and minerals, and these have an impact on our health. In this chapter, we describe these different types of nutrition so you can be an educated eater, *not* because you should eliminate particular foods from your **diet**, and *not* because you should feel guilty about what you eat.

FOOD'S "ENERGY VALUE"

Food is often described by how many calories it contains. A **calorie** is a unit of measurement that indicates the energy potential of a substance (it is also often written as **kilocalorie** or **kcal**). How much energy you need to get from your food depends on a lot of factors. Bigger people need more calories to keep their bodies running well. It's like heating a house: a bigger house needs more heat than a smaller house to keep it just as warm. If you're a very active person, you'll also need more calories to keep your body working because you burn energy or calories when you exercise. Boys and men also tend to need more calories than girls and women. However, focusing on specific calorie information is probably less important than focusing on eating nutritious foods and listening to your body's signals of hunger and fullness. So, what are nutritious choices and what aren't? The rest of the chapter provides an overview of some of the specifics.

FAT

Perhaps no nutrient is more confusing these days than **fat**. You've probably heard of fat as being mostly bad for you. Or maybe you've heard of **ketogenic diets**, which suggest it's healthiest to get most of your energy from fat. In other words, people who recommend ketogenic diets are saying that fat is good. If you're like most people, you may have no idea what to think about fat—how much to eat it or how much to avoid it.

This is what nutrition scientists currently know when it comes to fat. Without any doubt, fat is more calorie-dense than other food nutrients, such as protein. What this means is that if you eat just a little bit of something high in fat, like a small cookie, it

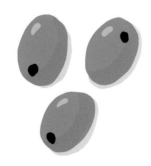

will likely contain a lot of calories. With that energy **density** comes a feeling of fullness, so if you eat something high in fat, you're likely to feel full faster and for longer than if you eat something that's low in fat. This can be good, especially if you know that you won't be able to eat again for many hours.

But if you're going to eat every few hours, or whenever you're hungry, do you need to consume fat? The answer is "yes," but it depends on what kind of fat you eat. There are different kinds of fat; for example, you may have heard that nuts contain "good fat" (unsaturated fat). Foods that contain **unsaturated fats**, such as nuts and avocados, can be good for your heart. In contrast, **saturated fats** such as butter, cream, cheese, and most meat, raise your **cholesterol** levels, which can be bad for your heart.

EXPERT ADVICE

Yaffi Lvova, *registered dietician nutritionist, USA*

"People often want to know how much they need to eat, but it's impossible to accurately calculate the amount of energy any individual needs on a given day. Calorie expenditure—the amount your body burns—relies not only on physical movement but also on the things you might not consider: digestion, breathing, even thinking. Even more than that, so many external factors account for the amount of calories your body will burn in a day: sleep quality and quantity, emotional and intellectual stress, hormones, and even the weather affect the energy you need in a day. And that's not even a complete list. Your body is the only calculator fancy enough to take all of that data and communicate it. That communication is your appetite. By allowing your appetite to lead the way, being sure to eat when you're hungry, and eating until you're full and satisfied, you will give your body the amount of energy it needs."

Eating fewer foods high in saturated fats can lower your **blood cholesterol**, which may lower your risk of some health problems later in life, including **heart disease** and some **cancers**. Eating fat is fine, unless you are eating a lot of food high in saturated fat all the time. Although your eating habits are unlikely to affect your health right now, it is valuable to establish good habits that will follow you into adulthood when you'll become more at risk of health problems such as heart disease.

The **bottom line** is that it's perfectly fine to consume foods containing fat, but try eating mostly foods that contain unsaturated fats. "Natural" foods (such as salmon, olives, and avocados) are likely to contain unsaturated fats, in contrast to **processed foods** (such as store-bought sweets or pizza), which are likely to contain saturated fats.

CARBOHYDRATES

Carbohydrates ("carbs") tend to have a bad reputation. In fact, some diets (for example, the Atkins and paleo diets) focus on reducing carbs in order to lose weight. However, it's nearly impossible to completely eliminate carbs from your diet and you shouldn't even try to.

Carbohydrates are an important part of your daily food intake for many reasons. Perhaps most important, carbs are an easy, fast source of energy for your body. This is partially why you may have heard of athletes "carb loading," or eating a lot of pasta before an athletic event. Having a lot of carbs in your system ready for use can support your athletic performance.

Carbohydrates are found in many different kinds of foods. Vegetables contain carbohydrates, as do pasta and cakes—a really wide range of foods have carbs in them. Like fats, not all carbs are alike, and some are more nutritious than others.

Plain white bread has a lot of carbs in it, but doesn't have much nutritional value and may contain processed ingredients that aren't especially healthy. Doughnuts combine carbs with fat (they're typically fried in oil), making them energy dense and high in saturated (less healthy) fat. So what carbs are best to eat?

Smart carbohydrate options include brown rice, oatmeal, and multigrain bread. Many fruits and vegetables (for example, apples and spinach) are also high in nutrients, and these carbohydrates have been found to help promote heart health.

The **bottom line** is that carbohydrates are a great source of energy for our bodies. According to the Mayo Clinic, a respected medical institution in the USA, nearly half of your diet should be made up of carbs. It's healthiest, however, to eat mostly the nutritious, unprocessed types of carbs found in fruits, vegetables, and whole grains.

PROTEIN

Protein is an important part of a balanced, healthy diet. Protein helps your bones, muscles, cartilage (soft, connective tissue found in the body), and skin to grow. It's also important for hormone functioning. Foods that are high in protein make you feel full more quickly than foods that are lower in protein. Eating protein is likely to keep you from feeling hungry. And, unlike some of the other nutrients discussed in this chapter, it's usually pretty easy to get the daily recommended amount of protein. According to the US Department of Agriculture, most people eat enough protein without even trying.

If you're looking to improve your nutritious food choices, think about adding healthy protein into your daily habits. Although most of us are likely to get protein from meats like hamburgers and chicken, there are other sources of proteins. Beans, peas, soy products (for example, tofu), nuts, and seeds are all excellent choices. Seafood such as salmon can also be a healthy way to increase the protein in your diet.

The **bottom line** is that protein is an important part of a healthy diet, but you're likely already eating plenty of protein, and eating "extra" protein will not lead to muscle growth. You may think about trying some new and different kinds of "lean proteins" that come from vegetables and other plants, and keep some of your meat protein to lean varieties like chicken.

MYTHS & MISBELIEFS

Boys and men need to eat more protein than girls.

This is a common misunderstanding. Boys and girls need approximately the same portion of protein in their diets, and they are likely getting enough protein without worrying about what they eat.

Information from the US National Health and Nutrition Examination Survey indicates that boys start to eat a lot more protein during their pre-teen and teen years. In fact, by early adulthood, men are usually eating too much protein and not nearly enough fruits and vegetables. Some of boys' interest in protein has to do with their belief that protein consumption will lead to muscle development or "bulking up." The body can only absorb so much protein, however. Overdoing protein consumption has no benefit in terms of muscle development or athleticism; it is just likely to fill you up and take the place of other important nutrients.

EXPERT ADVICE

Georgie Fear, *registered dietician, USA*

"If a teen boy is interested in gaining muscle, adding protein to his diet is usually not necessary. Muscle is built from doing strength exercises and eating enough food so your body has plenty of energy to build bigger muscles. Eating extra carbohydrates is a better way to get this extra energy."

SALT

Salt may be one of the most misunderstood substances in our diet. Salt is made up of the chemical compounds sodium and chloride, which are both essential to human survival. And yet you've probably heard people around you mention their desire to reduce their salt intake.

Salt (aka sodium on food labels) helps to preserve, or keep from going bad, many foods we consume and makes most foods taste better, so it's everywhere. Even food that doesn't taste salty often has salt in it, including most bread, pizza, and sandwiches. If you look through the fridge and cabinets in your house and read some food labels, you may be surprised. In one kitchen we found: one can of black beans = 120 milligrams (mg) of sodium, one piece of bread = 210 mg of sodium, one serving of mozzarella cheese = 170 mg of sodium, and one serving of chicken noodle soup = 700 mg of sodium. You can see how this adds up pretty fast.

Is there anything wrong with salt? Salt can contribute to water retention and constipation. More importantly, it has been associated with high blood pressure and heart disease. Because of this, the American Heart Association recommends that all of us keep our salt intake to around 1,500 mg per day. Most people consume 3,400 mg daily. One teaspoon of salt is approximately 2,300 mg of sodium.

Some doctors have recently found that the link between salt and heart health has been overstated. In fact, there may not be a lot of evidence to support switching to a low-salt diet. Because potassium helps rid your body of sodium, it may be better to *increase* your potassium intake. So what should you do? Probably nothing. Unless you know that high blood pressure and heart problems run in your family and it makes sense to be as cautious as you can be, you probably don't need to worry that much about your salt intake.

The **bottom line** is that salt makes food taste better and last longer, but it *may* be associated with high blood pressure and poor heart health when eaten in high amounts. Because scientists and doctors still don't fully understand the links between salt intake and health, the best thing to do may be to follow general health recommendations and try to include as many unprocessed, unpackaged foods in your diet as possible.

SUGAR

Did you know that the average American eats 22 teaspoons of **sugar** per day? Like salt, sugar sneaks into foods you wouldn't expect. Bread, chicken nuggets, granola bars, yogurt, and even ketchup are all surprisingly high in sugar. You may not realize that sugar comes in different forms: **high-fructose corn syrup**, cane sugar, **dextrose**, and fruit **juice concentrate**, among many others. This is one reason why you might not realize how much sugar you eat!

Most of the sugar we consume doesn't come right out of a container of sugar but is found in processed foods. Soda, juice, and some breakfast cereals are among the biggest culprits. Sugar is in many foods because it often makes them taste better. Unfortunately, as we all get used to eating packaged foods with a lot of sugar added, we seem to crave sugar more and more.

What's the problem with eating sugar? Sugar consumption has been linked to increases in weight in the last few decades, which isn't to say that eating some sugar and sugary foods is a problem. The biggest concern may be that eating processed, sugary foods is likely to take the place of healthier options. For example, a bowl of berries would be a **nutritious** and healthy dessert, but most of us would prefer to have those berries in a pie or on top of vanilla ice cream. The pie and ice cream would probably mean we'd eat fewer berries and more saturated fat (in the ice cream and piecrust). As Brennan's story suggests, it is easy to get into the habit of eating somewhat unhealthy foods, so try to make nutritious choices at least some of the time.

The **bottom line** is that it would be difficult to avoid all sugar and it isn't necessary to do so. It's a good idea, however, for the sake of your health, to sometimes avoid processed, sugary foods and stick to nutritious options like fruits and vegetables, which we'll discuss next.

Why is soda so bad for you? Is it OK to drink it sometimes?

You've probably heard a lot about soda being a bad beverage option. There are even taxes on soda in some cities in the USA, which make it cost more and encourages people to drink less. But what's all the fuss about? Can you drink soda sometimes?

Soda is often viewed as a problem for a few reasons: people tend to drink a lot of it, it has no nutritional health benefits, and it has a lot of sugar and calories. Furthermore, soda often takes the place of much healthier options like low-fat milk and water. Diet sodas don't contain any calories, so the concerns about their effect on weight is less of an issue. But keep in mind that diet sodas contain artificial sweeteners and chemicals that can hardly be called healthy.

Public health and policy officials often target soda because it has been linked to the increase in people's weight more than any other single food or beverage in recent years. Still, it's perfectly fine to drink soda occasionally. It's not a nutritious choice to make regularly, but a soda sometimes isn't going to hurt you.

MY STORY

BRENNAN MAURICE, 22 YEARS OLD

I've always been skinny and I've always been able to eat a lot. But lately, since I've finally stopped growing, I've been putting on some weight. I'm by no means overweight, but I have much more body fat than I'm used to and I would rather be thinner again. Since I left my job, which required a lot of manual labor, I've also lost a lot of the muscle mass I used to have, which I regret as well. I feel like I'm fat every time I weigh myself and it's higher than it was last time. These moments always leave me with shame and I'm trying to come to terms with my new body.

It probably doesn't help that I like to eat, and I like to eat things that taste the best, which are often the worst things for you. I feel guilty every time I eat junk food and often wish I were eating something healthier, but I tend to keep up the bad habit anyway. Since it's so convenient and inexpensive to eat something like fast food, it's often the thing I opt for rather that a homemade salad or something along those lines. I'd like to be better at actually eating healthier food rather than just wishing I ate healthier food.

I don't think anyone has ever said anything negative about my body to me, but I've had a few positive comments from friends and coworkers. I'm sure that positive comments from my friends across my adolescence reinforced my positive body image.

The best advice I can offer younger boys is to try and maintain a healthy and balanced diet and to exercise regularly. We're all going to grow up and our bodies change—sometimes in positive ways and sometimes in ways that feel less than positive—but being healthy is the most important.

FRUITS AND VEGETABLES

Most people don't eat enough fruits and vegetables, even though they know that they are among the most nutritious food options. In fact, it's nearly impossible to eat *too* many fruits and vegetables because they're such a good source of all kinds of nutrients.

The US Department of Agriculture recommends that half of *each* meal and snacks be made up of fruits and/or vegetables. Half! Although this may not seem realistic—you may not think that you have time to prepare fruits and vegetables for all your meals and snacks—fruits and vegetables should be a big part of our daily diet.

Why are fruits and vegetables this important? They contain important nutrients including folate, magnesium, potassium, fiber, vitamin A, vitamin C, and vitamin K. They also don't have the less healthy ingredients, such as preservatives, additives, salt, and sugars, that come with store-bought and packaged foods. It's also important to remember that fruits and vegetables can be delicious! You may want to explore new varieties and new ways of finding them, such as dried, frozen, or canned, and different ways of preparing them (for example, roasting and stir frying).

The **bottom line** is that fruits and vegetables are an important part of a healthy diet. Try to eat at least some sort of fruit and vegetable each day, and ideally at most meals.

MYTHS & MISBELIEFS

> Instead of eating fruit, it's just as healthy to drink fruit juice.

In recent years, juicing has become popular. This is just another way of saying "drinking juice" instead of eating solid foods. "Juicing" also refers to blending up fruits and vegetables in a blender and drinking them.

It's true that drinking nutrients can be faster and easier than eating them. If you're blending up fruits and vegetables at home, this may be a great way to drink nutrients. However, most store-bought juice isn't as healthy as the fruit (or vegetables) it comes from. For one thing, most juice contains added sugars to make it taste sweeter. Although there is nothing wrong with consuming some sugar (see the section above about sugar), it's healthier to eat the whole fruit without the sugar. Sometimes a *lot* of sugar is added to juice. In fact, some juices contain relatively little in the way of fruit or vegetables and as much sugar as a soda. In these cases, actual fruit and vegetables are much more nutritious than juice. Fruits and vegetables also typically contain some fiber, which is extracted when juice is made. Fiber has health benefits that make solid fruits and vegetables a better choice than juice.

The **bottom line** is that it's not true that drinking juice is typically as healthy as eating fruits or vegetables, and it may be worth checking the labels of the juices that you drink regularly. However, juice can be a healthy option, particularly if you make nutritious choices and opt for juices that are low in added sugar and other additives.

SUGAR

FIBER

Maybe you've heard the word **fiber**, but don't know exactly what it is. A food that is high in fiber is slowly digested by your body. That probably sounds weird, but there are actually (parts of) foods that pass through your body without really changing much. These foods tend to be bulky, filling, and come from natural (not processed) sources. Foods that are high in fiber include apples, artichokes, barley, beans, Brussels sprouts, carrots, citrus fruits, nuts, oats, peas, prunes, raspberries, wheat bran, and whole-wheat flour.

There are many benefits to eating foods high in fiber, including healthy digestion, lowered risk of **diabetes**, heart health, lowered cholesterol, healthy blood sugar levels, and regular bowel movements (it's better than the alternative—constipation!).

The **bottom line** is that including foods high in fiber, such as most fruits and vegetables, into your diet is good for your health in a variety of ways. These foods can also be delicious.

I know I don't eat nutritious foods most of the time, but I'm pretty thin and I feel fine. Do I need to try to change what I eat?

No one eats nutritious foods all the time, and it isn't necessary to, so you don't need to aim for all the time. With age, however, the association between how you feel, your weight, your health, and what you eat tends to become more apparent. The risks of a variety of chronic and serious illnesses such as diabetes and heart disease also increase with age, so what you eat becomes more important across adulthood.

This isn't to suggest that what you eat as a teen or young adult doesn't matter at all, because it does. One of the best ways to nurture your health and fuel physical fitness is to eat nutritious foods most of the time. Eating nutritious foods while you're young will also help you get into the habit of eating this way so that you can maintain good habits and good health into adulthood. Of course, everyone's body is different, and some of us are likely to notice more of a difference in how we feel based on what we eat.

VITAMINS AND MINERALS

Vitamins and minerals—otherwise known as micronutrients—are dietary components that your body needs in order to grow, develop, and stay healthy. Some of the most important micronutrients are iron, vitamin A, iodine, and zinc. The catch? These aren't produced in the body, but must be derived from food. Luckily, you don't need them in large quantities.

Most are easily available in foods and drinks you probably consume regularly. For example, most salt has iodine added to it, so you're most likely getting more than enough iodine. Vitamin A is important for your eyesight and immune system, but you're likely getting enough vitamin A in the milk you drink. If you don't drink milk, try kale; it's also full of vitamin A. Iron is important in keeping your brain and your muscles functioning well, and can be found in foods like lentils (and other beans), spinach, quinoa, most meat, tofu, and even dark chocolate. Zinc is good for your immune system and nervous system, and can be found in most meat, vegetables such as spinach, broccoli, and kale and in beans, lentils, nuts, seeds, and whole grains.

The **bottom line** is that, chances are, if you live in the USA or the UK, you don't have to worry about your vitamin and mineral consumption. You're likely getting what you need through the foods you eat.

MYTHS & MISBELIEFS

Taking vitamins and supplements will help you build muscle and improve your athletic performance.

As we described above, the vitamins and minerals that your body needs tend to be easily found in foods available to you. It is unlikely that you need to take vitamins and supplements (otherwise known as dietary supplements), which are intended to add to your diet when you are missing particular nutrients. You're probably not missing important nutrients! In fact, supplements can be more problematic than they are helpful, and you definitely don't need them to build muscle or increase fitness.

Although you may see advertisements for all sorts of supplements, including protein powder and weight-loss shakes, this does not mean that they are necessary or even healthy. In the USA, the **Food and Drug Administration (FDA)** monitors and approves food products and medications (aka drugs), but vitamins and supplements are not monitored. This means that many supplements are not tested to determine if they are helpful or safe before they are available to buy. When scientists examine these products, they often find them not to be helpful and to be potentially harmful. Some supplements have even been found to contain toxic or poisonous ingredients.

Other countries, such as the UK, *do* have agencies that monitor the safety of vitamins and supplements. This does not mean that these products are necessary or even healthy, but it does mean they are more likely to be safe. Still, you should avoid protein supplements and any sort of supplement that claims to help increase the size of your muscles. If you are interested in increasing your fitness, vitamins and supplements are not the answer!

SOME NUTRITIOUS FOODS TO TRY

There are so many wonderful, nutritious foods in the world. Some of them you may never have tried—and you should!

Food	Nutritious because...
Artichokes	High in fiber and healthy carbohydrates
Avocado	Contains healthy fats and carbohydrates
Brussels sprouts	High in vitamins C and K and fiber
Beets	High in fiber, potassium, and vitamin A
Cauliflower	High in vitamin C and fiber
Edamame/soybeans	High in protein and fiber
Greek yogurt	High in protein and calcium
Kale	High in vitamins A, C, and K, healthy carbohydrates, fiber, iron, and zinc
Mango	High in fiber, potassium, and vitamins A, B6 and C
Lentils	High in protein, fiber, vitamin B6, thiamin, magnesium, copper, iron, and zinc
Salmon	Contains healthy protein and fat, and high in vitamins B12 and D
Spinach	Contains healthy carbohydrates, protein, folate, magnesium, and vitamins A, C, and K
Sweet potatoes	High in fiber, potassium, and vitamins A and B6
Tofu	Contains healthy protein, fat, and iron
Walnuts	Contain healthy fat, protein, fiber, magnesium, potassium, vitamin B6

One of my friends always tells me that eating vegetarian food is "girly." Why is this? He seems to be suggesting that eating meat is "manly," but I don't understand why this would be.

It is possible that some people's ideas about meat being "manly" come from outdated ideas of men being the hunters or breadwinners in a society while women are the gatherers and caretakers (of children). It is not unusual to see advertisements for hamburgers or ribs that show muscular men eating large portions of meat. However, these advertisements rely on stereotypes about what men think (and how women view men) to sell products, so they should not be taken seriously.

Salads, tofu, and Impossible Burgers (aka vegetarian "burgers") are sometimes viewed as feminine foods, but these views also stem from outdated stereotypes of women being weak and dainty, while men are big and strong. Although meat is a valuable source of protein, both men and women need to eat other types of foods to support their health. Vegetables—including salads and "meat" products made from vegetables—can be incredibly healthy components of your diet.

If a friend suggests that it is important to eat meat to be a "real man," it's best to ignore this friend or just tell him that it is important to eat a variety of foods so that you can live a long and healthy life.

VEGETARIANISM, VEGANISM, PESCATARIANISM, AND OTHER -ISMS

Maybe you've heard about celebrities such as Ariana Grande, Brad Pitt, Beyoncé, Bruce Springsteen, and Kristen Bell choosing to eat vegan or vegetarian— at least for a little while. Many people consider eliminating meat from their diet at some point in their lives. Most **nutritionists** would agree that there are pros and cons to avoiding meat and other animal products. We'll briefly describe them here, define some terms, and give you a sense of what some of these different approaches to eating look like.

Vegetarians typically don't eat meat (for example, beef and pork), poultry (for example, chicken and turkey), or seafood (for example, salmon and shrimp). This may be a healthy choice for many people, as eliminating meat also removes a lot of saturated fat from most diets. There is evidence that the negative impact on the environment of raising animals for meat—beef in particular—is much more devastating than most people realize. Some people feel very strongly about not killing animals to provide a source of food for people. However, we also get a lot of nutrients from meat, seafood, and poultry; these foods can be very high in protein and iron (for example, in meat) and healthy fats (for example, in salmon). Human beings have been eating meat products since the beginning of recorded history, and there is likely a good reason for this. It's nutritious, filling, and can taste delicious.

Vegans are vegetarians who avoid all animal products. Not only do they not eat meat products, but they typically don't eat milk, cheese, eggs, and other **dairy** products. They also may avoid products that come from animals such as wool, silk, leather, and even honey. For some people, this may be a healthy way to eat, assuming they get plenty of nutrients from other foods such as nuts, beans, fruits, and vegetables. It also may be impractical. Some of your favorite foods would be eliminated from your diet if you became a vegan, including pizza, hamburgers, and fried chicken. Also, a lot of clothes and accessories are made of leather, such as belts and jackets, so it may be impractical for you to totally avoid animal products.

Pescatarians are vegetarians who eat seafood. For these people, seafood may be a favored food, or they may believe that the health benefits of eating seafood, and the lower environmental impact of producing seafood, make seafood an acceptable source of food. **Ovo-lacto vegetarians** (aka lacto-ovo vegetarians) are vegetarians who do eat eggs and drink milk. Actually, most vegetarians include eggs and milk in their diets, but sometimes, usually for people of certain religions such as Hinduism, this category is meaningful. **Flexitarians** are "sometimes vegetarians" who eat a mostly vegetarian diet. **Macrobiotic eaters** are vegans who only eat unprocessed foods and sometimes fish; they also avoid sugar and refined oils. As with vegetarianism and veganism, these types of eaters tend to want to improve their health and avoid animal suffering and unnecessary environmental damage.

Most of these types of diet require extra work and planning to ensure that you get enough of the nutrients needed, such as protein and iron. It can be inconvenient and impractical to give up the foods that most people eat. If you're interested in trying a vegetarian diet (or one of these other options), talk with the people you live with and see how they feel about this, and what they're willing to do to support you. Unless you do your own grocery shopping, it may be difficult to make drastic changes to your eating habits without the cooperation of others.

It's also important to keep in mind that eliminating meat (or some animal products) from your diet will not necessarily leave you eating more nutritiously; it depends on what you end up eating instead.

MY STORY

ANTHONY BROWN, 19 YEARS OLD

I feel confident in the way I look because, as an athlete, I've put a lot of time and effort into keeping myself healthy and fit. I started playing sports at age 4 and I've always tried to keep a positive sense of who I am and what I need to do to take care of myself.

I think it was probably around middle school when I realized I needed to take care of myself if I was going to be the best athlete I could be. When I was younger, it didn't really seem to matter what I ate or how much sleep I got; I felt able to perform at what I thought was my highest level. But sports get more competitive as you get older, and if you want to play well and not get hurt, you have to be more careful. I've tried to cut out soda and limit sweets in my diet. Instead, I've tried to eat healthier options such as yogurt, fruit, almonds, or celery with peanut butter.

As a hockey player and a runner, I don't expect that I'm ever going to look like Sidney Crosby (the hockey player) or like other professional athletes, but I want to look, feel, and perform my best.

If I was to offer my younger self advice, it would be to let him know that boys aren't really comfortable with their bodies. They don't seem to think about taking care of them the way that girls do. But eating well and being aware of what you need to do to look and feel good is important.

"MY PLATE"

Hopefully, after reading everything in this chapter, you understand that you can eat anything you want to, but that some foods have more health benefits than others. As Anthony's story reminds us, eating well will make you feel better and help you to be your best self. You can also see that the way that different foods (for example, fats) are talked about in public and online isn't always accurate. People can have very strong opinions about food, but this doesn't mean that these opinions are accurate.

The US government has offered a pretty basic way to think about what to eat if you're trying to be healthy. They call this **My Plate** (in contrast to "food pyramids" that kids of past generations were taught about), and there are a few things about it that are worth taking note of. First, the recommendation is for nearly half of each meal to be made up of fruits and vegetables. Second, the recommendation includes carbohydrates that are mostly grains (in other words, "healthy carbs"). Third, protein is an important component of a

healthy meal, but this may or may not be meat; there are many healthy sources of protein, such as beans and nuts.

Most people don't manage to put together each meal to include every healthy option. It's nice to have the goal of eating healthily, but it's a complicated and difficult goal. We'll discuss the importance of thinking about food in a flexible, balanced way in Chapters 7 and 8.

Summing Up #Nutrition101

- ☑ It's important to listen to your body and eat when you're hungry and stop when you're full.
- ☑ You can eat all foods, but do your best to eat foods that are nutritious, including a lot of fruits and vegetables.
- ☑ Eating nutritious foods is one important way to care for your body and develop a positive body image.

Find out more

- To learn more about intuitive eating, especially the basic ten principles, you might be interested in exploring this page on the website Intuitive Eating: www.intuitiveeating.org/10-principles-of-intuitive-eating/.
- The Mayo Clinic's web page has scientifically based information about nutrition, such as this page about carbohydrates: How carbs fit into a healthy diet, www.mayoclinic.org/healthy-lifestyle/nutrition-and-healthy-eating/in-depth/carbohydrates/art-20045705.
- To learn more about My Plate, visit www.choosemyplate.gov/.
- For more scholarly articles and web pages with information about healthy eating and nutrition, see the companion website for this book: www.TheBodyImageBookforBoys.com.

CHAPTER SEVEN

FORGET FOOD FADS

#EatWell

> "ALL YOU NEED IS LOVE. BUT A LITTLE CHOCOLATE NOW AND THEN DOESN'T HURT."
>
> Charles M. Schulz, American cartoonist, creator of Peanuts

Do you know or think about your weight?

Would you like to change what you weigh or how your body looks?

Can you change parts of your body by changing what you eat?

Guys are less likely to say they are on a "diet" than girls and women. However, they still often attempt to change their habits because they want to look bigger or leaner, and they think altering what they eat will help them accomplish their goals. A big part of why guys change their habits is because there is so much advertising that tries to convince us that we can change our body size and shape if we just follow a particular plan or buy a particular product. Most of this advertising and messaging offers nothing more than a **fad**—something that's popular for a short time, often for no obvious or scientific reason. **These fads are likely to cause more harm than good.**

In this chapter you'll learn

- ○ how to think about your height, weight, size, and shape in a way that is psychologically healthy,

- ○ why it's so difficult to change our body sizes and shapes, why food fads typically don't work, and why drastic measures can be disastrous, and

- ○ how to consider your eating habits, whether it makes sense to change them, and how this is relevant to your physical health.

YOU ARE WHO YOU ARE

There are a variety of factors that affect your height, body size, and shape, and many of them aren't within your control. One large scientific study found that at least 80% of the differences in height between you and your friends is due to your genes. In other words, you're however tall you are mostly due to

how tall your biological parents are. Differences between you and your friends in **nutrition**, medical care, and general health may affect your height a bit, but not a whole lot. A lack of protein *may* affect your height more than any other non-genetic factor, but as we discussed in Chapter 6, you are likely getting plenty of protein in your daily diet without trying. Eating more protein than your body needs won't help you grow taller.

Although weight is *somewhat* more easily changed than height, it's also very much influenced by our genes. Eating a variety of foods and a mostly nutritious diet is important for your long-term health, but trying to change your body size or shape by changing what you eat can be nearly impossible, and isn't always a good idea. Not only are our bodies' sizes and shapes mostly genetically determined—we can't change our genes—recent research suggests that our body size has a lot to do with our appetites, which are also determined by genetics. It can be hard to control appetite! Some people feel hungry more often and have a hard time eating less, even if they want to weigh less, and other people don't care as much about food because they don't feel hungry as often. Being hungry is a pretty miserable experience, and it's not a good idea to ignore hunger because you risk not only feeling very cranky, but also not giving your body the nutrients it needs.

PEOPLE ARE MORE THAN NUMBERS

OK, let's back up a bit. It's important to remember that your height and weight are just numbers. They may tell your doctor something about you—for example, when you were a little kid, your doctor probably wanted to make sure that you kept growing. If you didn't keep growing, it could have meant that there was a health issue your doctor needed to investigate. But your height and weight only say a little bit about your health and certainly do not determine your self-worth.

There has been a growing body of research suggesting that the links between weight (taking into account our height) and health are *really* complicated. Scientists and doctors have argued that people who are relatively heavy are at risk of health problems such as type 2 **diabetes**, heart disease, and some forms of cancer. However, it is

EXPERT ADVICE

Dr. Rebekah Fenton, *Lurie Children's Hospital/ Northwestern University Feinberg School of Medicine, USA*

"A weight in isolation doesn't tell us a lot about health. It doesn't indicate what percentage of the body is muscle or fat. It doesn't tell me if you've always been that weight or if you recently lost or gained weight. It especially doesn't let me know what you've done to get there. What you eat and what you do to keep your body active determine your health. As an adolescent medicine specialist, I center my conversations with patients around nutrition and activity, instead of weight, because they are better indicators of our present and future health status. My goal is to help teens learn to love themselves and take care of their body without introducing weight stigma."

becoming clear that there are many factors that contribute to our health aside from our weight. For example, if you exercise and are in good physical shape, you may improve your heart health. Eating foods that **nourish** our bodies is important so that we *feel good* and stay healthy. Getting enough sleep is also an important way to protect our health (discussed in Chapter 5), as is avoiding substance use problems (discussed in Chapter 9). There are many steps we can take to live a long, healthy life, and it is important to focus on behaviors we can change, instead of the things we can't, such as our height or body shape.

How often should you weigh yourself?

Unless you have a health condition that requires regularly monitoring your weight, then you don't need to weigh yourself very often. Depending on your age and whether or not you've completed puberty, it's normal to gain weight across your childhood and teen years. You're also getting taller and stronger, and gaining weight is a part of that. If you're curious about what you weigh, hopping on a scale once a month is more than sufficient. But don't spend a lot of time thinking about the number that appears on the scale. Your body and your health cannot be measured by just one number.

WHAT YOUR METABOLISM HAS TO DO WITH IT

Chances are you've heard people refer to their **metabolism** as "fast" or "slow." People seem to think that having a fast metabolism is a good thing, allowing them to eat more than those with a slow metabolism. There is no easy way, however, for most of us to know with any certainty about the complicated ways in which our bodies function.

It turns out that our metabolism—essentially, the chemical processes that take place within our bodies to keep us alive—changes. The biology that we're born with affects our metabolism, but so do our **behaviors**. In general, when we eat less food, our metabolism slows down and our body processes that food more slowly. It's like our bodies want to make good use of the smaller amount of food we're

MYTHS &
MISBELIEFS

When your doctor tells you that you need to lose weight, you should go on a diet.

Most doctors become doctors because they want to help people achieve good health and recover from illness or injury. They make recommendations that they believe will be helpful. However, most doctors receive very little (if any) training about nutrition, diet, body image, and weight. They can document where you fall on a height–weight chart, but they may not know much about how to educate and support their patients concerning eating and body image. In other words, although a doctor is a good person to turn to with questions about health and well-being, sometimes doctors may not be the best source of advice when it comes to your weight.

If you're ever told by a doctor that you need to lose weight, it's worth getting a second opinion from another medical professional. It may be most useful to talk with an expert who has been trained specifically to help people eat well and maintain a positive body image. A registered dietician, nutritionist, or even a psychologist with this specialty would be a good person to consult. If you live near a university, check to see if they have a center or clinic that helps people with concerns about their weight. Universities tend to be on top of the latest science, and sometimes even offer free health services to people interested in trying out new medical **regimens**.

Most importantly, if you believe—because a doctor told you so, or your own research leads you to believe this—that you need to lose weight, a food fad or any diet is not the answer. It may be a good idea to change your regular habits to eat more nutritious foods or to be more physically active, but only make changes that you plan to keep for the long term. As we'll explain more below, if you try a short-term diet or food fad of any kind, it's likely to lead to weight gain, not loss, over time. It's also likely to be a miserable experience.

offering them so they use it more slowly. Scientists believe that our bodies work this way because in ancient times it was difficult for people to find enough food to eat. When there was less food around (plants to grow and animals to catch and kill), our metabolism protected us by needing less food.

This isn't to say that we must always eat a lot to keep our metabolism working at full speed—it's not that simple. But we should listen to our bodies and eat what we need to feel full and energetic. If we try to eat too little, our bodies will process food slowly. This is one of the reasons why dieting to lose weight is so unlikely to work; our metabolism will work against our efforts. The best way to keep yourself and your metabolism happy is by properly nourishing yourself.

EXPERT ADVICE

Frank Bruni, journalist and op-ed columnist for *The New York Times*, USA

"When I was a teenager, I worried all the time about being wider than other kids or having love handles that they didn't or just being less firm, less flat. Because of that worry, I wanted to be comforted, and food comforted me, and I ate more and then I worried more about my body. It was an endless loop, and I could have broken free of it if I'd worked harder to put the worry aside, to focus on being healthy rather than being beautiful, and if I'd learned to see food as a source of strength and pleasure, but not as some blanket to be folded around me, some nursemaid for my emotions. We all judge ourselves more harshly than others judge us. Getting past that is a step toward liking your body better and having a better relationship with food."

WHAT EXACTLY ARE "FOOD FADS"?

When we talk about food fads, we are talking about any recommendation concerning how to eat that is not backed up by rigorous scientific studies. It turns out that just because you see information about a "juice cleanse" on TikTok, for example, does not mean that a juice cleanse is a good idea. Probably most of the information you see on social media about how to eat does not contain good ideas—in other words, ideas that are backed by scientific evidence. An influencer, or even some dieticians, may recommend food fads. Body image researchers often refer to all of these fads and messages suggesting that we should change our bodies as "diet culture."

How to spot a food fad

If a celebrity, influencer, or even a doctor describes an approach to eating using any of the below, it's likely to spell trouble:

- Results will be fast and easy to achieve!
  - We all like the idea of feeling or looking better quickly, but changing our habits to feel or look different usually takes months, or even years.
- It works for everyone!
  - We are all unique and a simple one-size-fits-all approach to health is rarely possible. We all need different amounts of food and have different preferences in terms of what we eat and the physical activities we participate in.
- Just buy my....
  - If a product is being sold, be suspicious. You don't need protein bars or juice blends to improve your health, lose weight, or gain muscle mass.
- The ingredients are "clinically proven" or "a proprietary blend."
  - If a product doesn't offer information about how it is tested to ensure that it is safe and effective, or if it refers to its ingredients as secret or "proprietary" (which means that the recipe is owned by the creator and will not be shared), walk the other way.

THE PROBLEMS WITH DIETS AND OTHER FOOD FADS

Most people will diet or try a food fad at some point because they hope to change how they look. Maybe you've seen this in your home, with your mom, dad, brother, or sister trying something like Weight Watchers (now called WW) or **intermittent fasting** (sometimes called IF; we discuss intermittent fasting more in Chapter 8). Maybe you've even tried a food fad yourself, such as trying not to eat any sugar. Food fads are surprisingly common, despite the fact that they don't work in the long run and they aren't backed by science. It's important to understand what scientists know surrounding food fads and dieting so you can make good choices about how you eat and the physical activity that you participate in for the rest of your life.

HOW DO YOU KNOW IF IT'S A FAD? WHAT'S THE BIG DEAL IF IT IS?

If something sounds too good to be true, it probably is!

If you see something online suggesting that it will "cleanse" or "detox" you, it's probably a fad. We have a natural system for detoxification; our kidneys remove waste products and excess fluid from the body. We do not need to use a product or follow a plan to cleanse or detox our bodies. We also do not need to eat "clean" food or "guilt-free" food. No food is "dirty" (unless it literally has dirt on it!), and no food should cause you to feel guilty. These are **advertising** tricks to make us feel like we should eat certain things or buy certain products. As we discussed in Chapter 6, a healthy diet can include eating all sorts of foods. Finally, you'll know it is a fad if you're told that a product or plan will "melt fat." Although it may seem appealing to just watch the fat melt off your body, this is not at all how our bodies work.

There are many problems with food fads. They are likely to encourage extreme habits and unhealthy behaviors, and they are unlikely to offer a long-term approach to taking care of your health. Below, we discuss six specific reasons to avoid food fads.

1. They don't work. In fact, they're likely to backfire.

Let's say you decide to try a "fat melting, low-carb diet." You cut out most bread, pasta, and other grain-based foods from your diet. You'll miss those foods a lot! Assuming you replace those foods with nutritious meats and fats, you may initially feel good and you may lose weight. For most people (including the thousands of people who have been studied), the feeling good/weight loss part of this experience lasts a few months, maybe 3 months if you're lucky. And then life gets in the way and willpower falls short.

You'll be out to dinner with friends and you won't be able to resist the rolls. Your dad will make your favorite pasta dinner and you'll eat three servings. You'll have a bad day at school and you'll eat a bagel for lunch. Gradually, the carbs will sneak back into your diet (as they should), and gradually, you'll gain whatever weight you lost. In studies that follow people across time, nearly *everyone* who followed a plan that eliminated entire groups of food (carbohydrates, fats) gained back the weight they lost after 2 years, and most gained extra weight, too.

2. Food fads will make you cranky.

When people commit to a food fad, they often claim that they want to feel better. People usually expect to feel better both physically and psychologically. Research suggests that people often do feel good at the start. They tend to feel like they're committing to do something for themselves that's important.

The problem? These good feelings don't last very long, because none of us like to be deprived. If we've decided to avoid sugar, for example, we'll end

up feeling irritable that we aren't able to eat sugar. Although this change to your diet was intended to make you feel better, within a few days you may actually feel worse.

One of the first studies to examine this phenomenon took place in the 1940s. The scientists conducting the study drastically reduced the food that participants could eat and people lost weight. That was expected. What wasn't expected was how this experiment affected the participants' mental health. They became obsessed with food and some even began to dream about food. They had a hard time focusing on regular activities and they became more socially withdrawn, **depressed**, and very, very cranky. Recent studies confirm these early findings: food fads and diets aren't good for your **mental health**.

3. They encourage body hate.

The diet and supplement industry attracts so many customers because it manages to convince us that there is something wrong with our bodies. The industry tells us there is something wrong with us—we're too skinny, too heavy, or not muscular enough—but they can help us fix it. Fads focus us on what we shouldn't do (and shouldn't eat) in order to be more attractive. This is an unhealthy way to think about ourselves.

A different way to think about our bodies is in a loving, caring way, which means thinking about the things we *want* to do to take care of ourselves, not the activities and foods we want to avoid. Psychologists have done research on goal-setting and have found that goals such as this, focusing on what we *do* want to do, are usually easier to achieve than "avoidance goals" (as they're sometimes called). This is a much healthier way to think about our bodies. Focusing on our health and nourishing our bodies is an important component of self-care. Plus, body hate is a waste of energy and is generally unhelpful.

DECLAN AUGUST, 23 YEARS OLD

I like my body, but wish I was able to build more muscle and tone it. I've also felt like I've been putting on weight lately. Not a ton of weight, probably around 10 pounds. I was the same weight for a few years, so I was used to how my body looked and felt. I am slowly getting more comfortable with how I look now, but it will take some time.

I exercise semi-regularly. When I get home from work, I am usually unmotivated to work out, but when I am in the mood, I won't hesitate to exercise. I run (weather permitting) and this helps me get most of my energy out and break a good sweat.

There have been a few athletes I've heard talking about the importance of eating a balanced diet and drinking a lot of water. This has really stuck with me in the past couple of years and I've realized that I do notice a difference when I eat mostly healthy foods and drink water compared with when I don't. When I don't eat well, I notice that I feel groggy, tired, and a little depressed. I just don't feel myself when I've been eating like total crap. I try to have a balanced diet so I can still treat myself, but feel great.

As I've gotten older, I am more conscious about what I need to do to feel well and also to look my best. I've also come to appreciate that you can learn to love your body and learn to love putting in the work it takes to look and feel how you want to. Judging your looks based off other's looks is silly when you think about it. And at the end of the day *you* are not *them*. This is especially the case with social media; you are usually seeing what *they* want you to see. Social media can really affect how you view yourself and can make you feel bad about yourself and not love your body. It is important to take a step back and realize what is real and what isn't.

4. Fads and diets use up valuable brainpower.

Although we all have the potential to keep learning throughout life and to continue to get smarter, our brains can only do so much at a time. Even if you're an excellent multi-tasker, you probably can't cook a meal while reading a book while having a conversation with someone else. You can only think about and do a couple of things at a time. If you're focusing a lot on what you can or can't eat—eating being something you likely do throughout the day—this is going to distract from other things that you could (and possibly should) be doing. Sometimes scientists refer to this as "attentional focus" or "bandwidth." As you grow up and you find yourself tempted by all sorts of fads and diets, it's worth keeping in mind that deciding to follow a fad means deciding not to do other things, or not do other things as well as you could have. Is this a choice you want to make?

EXPERT ADVICE

Oona Hanson, *educator and health advocate, USA*

"When it comes to social media and advertising, be prepared to notice—and push back against—the fitness and wellness industry's attempts to make boys feel bad about their bodies. Old-school diet companies used to target only girls and women, but now this multi-billion-dollar industry is trying to capture the attention of the other half of the population. So rather than selling products only with images of an idealized female 'bikini body,' companies now feature hyper-muscular male physiques and use language like 'biohacking' and 'optimizing performance.' It's essential to bring your critical thinking skills—and a skeptical eye—when an influencer is trying to profit from body insecurities they themselves helped create!"

5. Ironic processing.

Have you ever tried not to think about something and found that you couldn't get it out of your mind? Maybe you were irritated with a friend and you tried to clear your mind of this irritation to focus on a test at school, but it kept creeping back into your mind. Ironic processing is the scientific term used for when you're trying to clear your mind of a thought, but it actually seems to have the opposite effect and you often find yourself thinking about it more. (It's "ironic" because it's the opposite of what you'd expect, and the "processing" part refers to your thoughts or "cognitive processes.") How is this related to what you eat? Well, a lot of food fads and diets are all about trying to not eat foods that you like and probably want to eat. The more you try to not think about these foods, the more you may actually want them!

Don't believe us? You can try a little experiment on your own. Try not to think about anything chocolate for the next two minutes. You can watch a clock to keep track of time and just sit still, relax, and try not to think about chocolate—cake, cookies, ice cream—put it all out of your mind. How did that turn out?

6. Diet plans and products (such as supplements) are part of a "for-profit" industry.

Maybe you've heard of "non-profit" organizations. A non-profit organization has a goal to help the world in some way, such as the Red Cross, which is dedicated to disaster relief. These organizations don't aim to make money, and any money they obtain through donations or fundraising is used to further the organization's goals.

The diet and supplement industry is **not** a non-profit industry. Many products and plans are described as "prescriptions for health," and opportunities to feel better. We tend to associate health organizations with non-profit organizations and think of medical providers and medical plans as having the goal of helping us get healthier. But this isn't how fads and diet plans work.

The diet and supplement industry is a multi-billion-dollar industry. People who come up with and sell diet plans don't necessarily care about your health, and they don't necessarily care if you lose weight or gain weight— they care about making money. If your body or weight doesn't change in the way you'd like it to, you may need their "product" again that much sooner.

This may sound cynical, but some have gone as far as to say that the dieting industry is the only profitable industry in the world with a 98% failure rate. Keep this in mind the next time you're tempted to follow a fad: there are a lot of people who would be very happy to have you buy their products and plans, and pay for their book or other services. This doesn't mean they have your best interests in mind.

Q+A

I've heard of the Health at Every Size Movement (HAES) and I don't understand how that works. Can you explain HAES?

The Health at Every Size movement (HAES) is an anti-diet, body positivity, diversity acceptance movement. HAES suggests that it's important for people to focus on healthy behaviors, no matter what their size. The idea is to not confuse the way people look and their health. There is so much that contributes to health that you can't just look at someone and decide they are unhealthy.

The HAES philosophy is consistent with the evidence and ideas presented in this book. There is scientific evidence that links weight and health, although these links are complicated and not completely understood. Regardless, not every larger person will have health problems, and many people who are smaller may have health problems. Every person should respect, appreciate, and do what they can to take care of their body.

Importantly, the HAES movement reminds us that all people deserve to be treated with kindness and should not be discriminated against because of their size. We all should care about our health more than we care about looking like our favorite celebrities or Instagram influencers. HAES also presents a really important counterpoint to all the fads and diets out there that can be incredibly harmful. The more we are self-accepting and supportive of others' self-acceptance, the easier it will be for all of us to reject these fads.

MYTHS & MISBELIEFS

Weight-loss apps and activity trackers are the best way to improve your eating habits and get fit.

Today's technology provides us with many different types of apps and fitness trackers. At first glance, you'd suspect that they would help us monitor our eating and activity habits—and change them for the better. However, the research suggests that this is not necessarily the case.

In one study of people trying to lose weight, some people wore trackers and some didn't. It turned out that the group who wore activity trackers were actually less likely to lose weight. In another study that examined the popular app MyFitnessPal, which tracks food intake and activity, people who used the app were compared with those who didn't. After 6 months, the groups were basically the same in terms of weight loss. Other research suggests that keeping track of what you eat may have benefits because it can be valuable to know how much you are actually eating and moving (we are not very good at remembering this on our own).

Activity trackers and fitness apps are part of a multi-million-dollar business and are likely to be around for a long time, but should you use them? If you feel that you may find an activity tracker or a fitness app helpful, you could try to use one. However, you don't want your eating and activity habits to feel like homework. Food and physical activity should be fun. Be honest with yourself about whether or not using an activity tracker or fitness app takes away from your enjoyment of eating and exercising, and don't be afraid to discontinue your use if your answer is "yes."

DO THIS INSTEAD

1. Focus on your health.

When you become a teenager, you start to become more responsible for your own health. You also probably have more freedom in terms of what you eat and how you spend your time. It is natural to want to take advantage of that freedom and you may find yourself eating fast food or drinking soda or doing other things your family may not have allowed previously. No one has perfectly healthy habits all the time and no one should worry if they stop at McDonald's occasionally. You may find, however, that you do not feel your best if you stop at McDonald's every day. You may also find that you feel better when you are active and get plenty of sleep. If you've fallen away from routines that make you feel good and are good for your body and mind, it is OK to try to change your habits.

It's critically important that you focus on your health and avoid fads when it comes to food. If you want to change your habits—concerning food, exercise, or anything, really!—be sure you are making changes that are backed by science.

2. Make small, sustainable changes.

The biggest mistake people tend to make when they decide to change a health habit is that they aim too high and don't focus on *sustainable* goals. In other words, people aren't always very good at being honest with themselves about their current habits and about the likelihood of maintaining their desired goals. You're better off making small changes to your habits that you can actually stick with. For example, if you drink juice or soda regularly, you could switch to water or milk most days. It might be hard at first, but once you are in the habit, you may realize that soda doesn't even taste that good to you anymore. Because soda doesn't add any nutrients to your diet, this is a positive health swap. However, this also doesn't mean that you can *never* drink soda!

Behavioral science research supports the approach that we recommend. Making small, sustainable changes to your health habits is far better than trying to cut out all sugar or carbs or count every single calorie. Most people would improve their health if they just ate one more piece of fruit or one more vegetable per day. Most people would feel better if they exercised for even 15 minutes more per day. These sorts of small changes to our lives are not necessarily fast ways to feel better or become healthier. Sometimes it takes days, weeks, or even months to notice any changes as a result of changing small habits. Be patient! Remember, your primary goal is to improve your health and how you *feel*. Being happy, healthy, and confident is important for the rest of your life, and these factors are all part of maintaining a positive body image.

SPORTS AND FOOD

In a recent study, about two-thirds of boys said that they changed their eating habits because they wanted to increase their muscle size or tone. If you are an athlete or interested in becoming one, you may be especially likely to experience some pressure to have a certain body type. If you are a wrestler, you may experience pressure to lose weight. If you want to play rugby or American football, you may feel pressure to gain weight. Although we understand why this may lead you to consider trying a fad diet or other approach to eating—don't do it!

It's important to remember the information we provided at the start of this chapter about the genetic and biological influences on our height, weight, size, and body shape. Some research indicates that the average man (in the U.S. or U.K) is 5' 9–10" tall (175.26–180.34 cm) and weighs about 182 pounds (82.55 kilograms or kg). In contrast, the average professional American football player is 6'

You've said that if you're hungry, don't ignore it. My mom tells me I'm just bored sometimes and not hungry. How do I know the difference?

It's likely that we all eat sometimes because we are bored and not hungry. Or maybe we're happy or want to celebrate so we eat. There isn't necessarily anything wrong with this. It's OK to just feel like something sweet and eat some ice cream, even though we aren't really hungry.

We discuss intuitive eating more in Chapter 6, but we'll mention it here because it is relevant to answering this question. If you eat intuitively, you listen to your body's signals of hunger and fullness and you trust your body to let you know when you need food. Because our modern lives don't always allow us to eat exactly when we first notice we're hungry (maybe that's not when you have a lunch period at school or when your parents have dinner ready), we sometimes have to ignore our stomach when it starts to growl. But do your best to listen to your body and let it guide you. Especially as you go through puberty and are growing, your stomach may not always seem to make a lot of sense. You may be really hungry some days and less hungry other days, but do your best to pay attention to your body. If your mom suggests you aren't hungry when you're sure that you are, you could always suggest that you'll eat a piece of fruit. We don't know many moms who would oppose that!

2" tall (187.96 cm) and weighs almost 250 pounds (113.4 kg). The average professional basketball player is 6' 7" tall (200.66 cm) and weighs 222 pounds (100.7 kg). In other words, professional athletes have bodies that tend to be pretty different from the average person. This isn't to say that you will never be an athlete if you don't have the "right" body type for your sport.

Stephen Curry has been called the greatest shooter in the history of the National Basketball Association, but he is 6' 3" (190.5 cm) and weighs under 200 pounds (90.72 kg). Darren Sproles was an American football player at 5' 6" (167.64 cm) 185 pounds (83.91 kg); he's currently ranked fifth in career all-purpose yards in the National Football League's history.

Trying to change your body for your sport is likely to be unsustainable and may even put your health at risk. Of course, you can eat nutritious food, work out, and do exercises to increase your strength. However, everything else we discuss in this chapter about avoiding food fads and diets is relevant to athletes as well—especially because to be an athlete means that you need to take care of your body so that it can be in tip-top shape!

STAY STRONG

Someday you'll see a food fad or a diet and be tempted to try it. Unfortunately, the odds are against us avoiding these fads, because they're constantly marketed to us. There's always something new, something that promises to really work this time. It may seem easy, so you'll think, "What's the harm? Why not give it a try?"

You may be tricked into trying something because it sounds scientific. Or because no one calls it a "diet." It's a "juice cleanse," which is going to make you healthier. Maybe it's a "sugar fast," and you know that sugar isn't particularly nutritious. But all of these things are different kinds of fads. The main reason they won't work is because they aren't sustainable. You won't want to only drink juice forever, and you won't want to give up sugar forever, so eventually you'll go back to your old habits from before you were trying to "cleanse" or "fast." Instead of falling for the latest fad, it's important to stay strong and focus on your health.

One final thought: When we spend time and energy thinking about our bodies and our weight, this is time and energy taken away from other things we could be doing, and we all only have a limited amount of time and energy in each day. It's important that we think about what's most important to us and how we want to spend our time and energy.

SEAN CAMS, 18 YEARS OLD

I love my body now, but I used to hate it when I was younger. There was a tradition in my school for the 5th grade end-of-year celebration that includes a pool party at the local pool. A part of the celebration is for someone to belly flop off the diving board to start off the fun. I volunteered myself to do the belly flop. I jumped off the board and as I hit the water, pain surged through my belly. I heard cheers as I breached the surface and I was greeted by a circle of my classmates after I got out of the water. All of them were grabbing flabs of my belly and chest and shrieking about how red it was. That was the first time I ever felt truly uncomfortable in my own skin.

I used to have "man titties," as my friends described them. One time, I saw an ad online for women with big boobs. The product was basically tape that could be used to make your chest seem smaller. A light bulb went off in my head. The next day I went into school with my chest taped up. This ingenious idea had no true visual effect and was just a sweaty, sticky, Scotch Tape mess when I got home. After hitting rock bottom that day, I began to accept my body more and more.

I've been a Rocky (i.e. Sylvester Stallone) fan since before I can remember. I love the movies and I've always been intrigued by Stallone's big chest and shoulders and chiseled core. In the past year, I've started to lift weights and I fantasize about looking like Stallone. Even though I know it is an impossible goal, it's still motivating.

My sister has also been an inspiration in my own journey to be more accepting of myself. She struggled with a pretty serious eating disorder for a few years. Watching her go from skin and bones to a much more psychologically and physically healthy place has taught me a lot. It's hard not to have body image issues with guys like Stallone in the movies and influencers on social media telling you to work out. I've come to understand, however, that the voice inside your head is always your biggest critic. You have to ignore that voice if you're going to be comfortable with yourself.

Summing Up #EatWell

- ✓ Your height, weight, size, and shape are unlikely to be changed in a positive way by following a particular diet or food fad such as a "cleanse."

- ✓ Following food fads and diets is likely to make you cranky, and they aren't good for your body image, mental well-being, or physical health.

- ✓ Focusing on your health, changing your habits slowly, and trying to incorporate more nutritious foods like fruits and vegetables into your daily routine are much better for you than following unscientific food fads.

Find out more

- The Centers for Disease Control and Prevention and the World Health Organization have web pages that include information about how to understand your weight. Check out: www.cdc.gov/nccdphp/dnpa/ growthcharts/resources/growthchart.pdf.

- To learn more about how to eat without dieting, fads, or "food rules," check out *Intuitive Eating (A Radical Anti-Diet Approach)* (2020) by Evelyn Tribole and Elyse Resch. Publisher: St. Martin's Essentials.

- For more information about the Health at Every Size Movement (HAES), check out *Body Respect: What Conventional Health Books Leave Out, Get Wrong and Just Plain Fail to Understand about Weight* (2014) by Linda Bacon and Lucy Aphramor. Publisher: BenBella Books. You may also want to check out Linda Bacon's new book, *Radical Belonging: How to Survive and Thrive in an Unjust World* (2020). Publisher: BenBella Books.

- For more scholarly articles and web pages with information about healthy eating and nutrition, see the companion website for this book: www.TheBodyImageBookforBoys.com.

CHAPTER EIGHT

LOVE TO EAT

#KeepFoodFun

"LAUGHTER IS BRIGHTEST
WHERE FOOD IS BEST."
Irish proverb

It would be easy to read Chapters 6 and 7 and think that eating is pretty complicated. Maybe you already thought that. Eating well may seem difficult because our scientific understanding is always improving, and with new research we discover more about nutrition and health. But in a lot of ways, eating isn't—or shouldn't be—hard. It is healthy to enjoy eating and our goal for you is to think positive thoughts about food.

In this chapter you'll learn

○ why it's important to be thoughtful about your food choices and to enjoy food,

○ what defines **eating disorders** and how they can develop, and

○ how to improve your way of thinking about food and adopt habits to support a positive body image.

BALANCE AND MODERATION

In some ways, healthy eating is simple. Eat when you're hungry. Stop eating when you're full. Try to eat fruits and vegetables and limit the amount of sweet and fatty foods. The problem with this logical, healthy advice is that we often have feelings about food. We crave a cheeseburger when we're hungry. We want our mom's chicken noodle soup when we're sick. We eat an entire container of Ben and Jerry's ice cream when we're sad. We're not always logical and sensible when it comes to food.

It's OK to give in to these emotions surrounding food. An occasional tub of ice cream isn't going to kill you. But a tub of ice cream every day is probably not the best habit. As you get older and you eat more independently—choosing your own lunches at school or choosing what you eat when you are

out with friends—it's important to try to be balanced and moderate in your choices. By balanced, we mean that you eat a variety of foods and don't overdo those that are not especially nutritious. By moderate, we mean that you don't take your eating habits to extremes. Choose fries at school some days, but not every day. Sometimes opt for a grilled chicken sandwich instead of the cheeseburger. Have a small serving of ice cream some days and an ice cream sundae less often. There is no reason to feel bad about what you eat; food should be a positive in your life and not a source of angst or shame.

LIVE TO EAT

Some research has been done that involves showing the words "chocolate cake" to Americans and French people. For Americans, the phrase brings "guilt" to mind, while the first word that comes to mind for the French is "celebration." Our goal for you is to think about chocolate cake (assuming you like chocolate cake) as wonderful and to be enjoyed, not a source of guilt. Food can be an extremely pleasurable part of our lives and it is important that concern for "healthy" eating does not drain the pleasure food can provide.

Sometimes people eat out of boredom without enjoying the process of meal planning and eating. This is referred to as **mindless eating**, which can lead to negative consequences, including overeating, guilt, and loss of enjoyment surrounding one of life's greatest pleasures. Think about it this way: if you sit in front of the television and eat an entire bag of chips while watching a show, you'll no longer be hungry. However, you probably won't have paid very much attention to what you were eating, and you probably won't have savored or enjoyed those chips. (**Savoring** means really noticing and enjoying what you taste.) After eating that entire bag of chips, you may feel too full and guilty about eating so much of something that you know isn't especially nutritious. But if you put a handful of chips in a bowl and eat them slowly, and with less distraction (not in front of the television), you'd probably enjoy them a lot more. Not only would you have a more positive eating experience, you'd probably end up eating less; more isn't always better.

Because we equate eating with guilt in many Western cultures (such as the USA and the UK), and because we spend a fair amount of energy thinking about how much and what we're eating, we miss out on a lot of the fun and enjoyment that food could bring us. Many of us have grown up thinking of some foods as "good" and some foods as "bad." I bet you could list five "good" and five "bad" foods without any trouble. Maybe you'd have milk, apples, broccoli, carrots, and Greek yogurt on your good list. Maybe you'd have French fries, pizza, ice cream and sweets and chocolate on your bad list. But is food really this straightforward?

There are a number of reasons why it's problematic to think of foods as "good" and "bad." First of all, most foods contain many different nutrients, so they're rarely entirely bad or entirely good. Second, when you feel that a food is bad and forbidden, it can make you want that food that much more. Imagine what would happen if your mom repeatedly told you that you must eat ice cream for dinner if you wanted broccoli for dessert? You might start to think that broccoli must be pretty awesome if you had to earn it by eating ice cream, and that ice cream must not be all that great. In other words, how we think about and label food can change how much we want it. Also, when we label food as "bad," we're more likely to feel guilty for eating it. This label can change how much we enjoy food—in particular, the

foods that are often meant to be special, or a part of celebrations. If your mom makes you a delicious chocolate cake for your birthday, enjoy it and relish this part of celebrating your special day. Don't feel guilty or think of your cake as "bad."

MY STORY

JAMES MATTHEW, 20 YEARS OLD

I've always been somewhat self-conscious about my body, never to the point where I feel embarrassed of it or afraid to take my shirt off in the appropriate settings (beach, swimming pool, etc.), but at times I've wished I looked better.

I give some thought to what I eat, but I'm such a big fan of food that it overrides these thoughts sometimes. Not to the point where I'm gorging myself on junk foods at all hours of the day, but I will eat a piece of cake, or a cookie, even if I'm not really hungry. I think this is because I am not completely unhappy with my body and would rather eat the foods that I enjoy eating.

I think that athletes mostly influence my sense of what a man should look like. Being an avid sports fan, I'm constantly watching people in peak physical condition, and that's probably the thing that motivates me to continue exercising enough to where I don't allow myself to become overweight or obese. I play basketball a lot, just recreationally. This makes up the majority of the time I spend working out or exercising. It's difficult for me to motivate myself to lift weights or go to the gym because I don't really enjoy myself there, whereas I'm always able to have fun running around playing basketball at my school gym.

My best advice for younger guys would be to live the lifestyle that you want to live. Don't let other people determine your feelings about your body. If you're happy with the way it is, then fine, keep it that way. If you are unhappy with it, change it. Life is too short to look a certain way for the sake of others.

BIGGER AND FASTER ISN'T ALWAYS BETTER

According to the Centers for Disease Control and Prevention (CDC), more than one in three Americans eat fast food each day. Fast food is typically relatively inexpensive and filling. However, research indicates that people in both the USA and the UK who consume fast food regularly tend to weigh more.

Of course, there is nothing wrong with wanting food fast—especially if you are hungry! But getting food from a drive-through, eating in our cars, and eating food prepared outside the home (which tends to be less healthy) on a regular basis aren't the best habits. Eating fast food tends to contribute to mindless eating and rarely lends itself to sit-down, family-style dinners, and savoring our food.

In addition to wanting our food fast, we also tend to want as much as we can get for as little money as possible. We tend to value quantity (how much) over quality (how tasty/nutritious the food is). Of course you don't have to eat all the food on your plate at home or given to you at any restaurant, but research suggests that bigger portion sizes lead people to eat more. It's better for you to eat nutritious, tasty, fresh food in smaller quantities than it is to eat a lot of food that isn't particularly nutritious, tasty, or fresh.

In many countries, such as Italy, food is viewed as nearly sacred. Planning what to eat, preparing food, and sharing it with others

is an important part of people's daily ritual. People in Italy don't eat more than people in the USA or the UK—in fact they typically eat less—but they enjoy food more. We think that's some pretty important food for thought.

REMINDER: RESTRICTION IS NOT RIGHT

It's important to enjoy eating nutritious foods. It's equally important not to be too rigid about your food choices. As we discussed in Chapter 7, it can backfire if you spend too much energy trying to avoid the foods you love.

There are a variety of potentially negative consequences of denying yourself foods that you enjoy. Aside from not being able to enjoy food, you may miss out on a lot, because food is often an important part of social and cultural experiences. A birthday cake or a wedding cake is considered an important part of the celebration. A big turkey or ham dinner is an important part of Thanksgiving or Christmas gatherings. Hotdogs, hamburgers, and pies can be favorite parts of a backyard barbecue in the summer. These gatherings and celebrations are about the time spent with loved ones, the holidays, and the memories made. They are also, for many people, about the food. Of course, you can go to a barbecue and not eat a hamburger. However, if you spend the entire gathering avoiding hamburgers, feeling deprived, and wishing you could eat a hamburger, you aren't going to have a lot of fun. At the extreme, consistent food restriction can lead to the development of an eating disorder.

MYTHS & MISBELIEFS

> **Eating disorders do not affect boys.**

This is a really dangerous misbelief that seems prevalent in popular culture. **Eating disorders *do* affect boys and men and can be really serious**. We'll discuss eating disorders more below, but we want to explain a bit about why many people have this misunderstanding about boys, men, and eating disorders.

Eating disorders were not really discussed much in the medical and psychological communities before the 1980s, and our understanding of these disorders has changed and evolved a lot in the past 40 years. In the beginning, these disorders were viewed as only likely to occur among adolescent girls, but we now know this is not true. Boys and girls, children and adolescents, and men and women all may develop an eating disorder.

Part of the reason that eating disorders were identified typically among teen girls has to do with the behaviors and symptoms that psychologists and doctors were looking for at the time: **fasting** (food refusal) and **purging** (for example, throwing up after eating). We now have a better understanding of the many behaviors and symptoms that may comprise an eating disorder, including over-exercise, supplement use, and **binge** eating. Some of these behaviors are more common among boys who have eating disorders than they are among girls. Recent research suggests that eating disorders may be increasing at a faster rate among males than among females. Celebrities such as Zayn Malik (from the band *One Direction*) and the rapper Eminem have struggled with eating disorders, and it's likely that people you know have as well. One report suggests that 25% of people with eating disorders are male.

It's really important to remember that food should be a positive part of our lives. If it is a source of stress, or if behaviors concerning food, weight, or body image are interfering with someone's happiness, then it is important for them to get help.

Q+A

Is food addiction an eating disorder? Can you be addicted to foods like sugar? Can you be a chocoholic?

Food addiction isn't considered an eating disorder by psychologists. Addictions can be extremely serious and even deadly, but usually when psychologists discuss addictions, they refer to chemicals or substances like nicotine found in cigarettes, or alcohol or drugs. Regular overuse of these substances can affect nearly every part of the body and result in a physical dependency on them. In other words, once a person is used to regular drug use, for example, they'll experience withdrawal symptoms when the drug use stops. The person comes to need the drug, and without it they may experience symptoms ranging from flu-like symptoms and seizures to headaches and shaking. Although eating less of a food you're used to eating regularly may result in cravings, it's unlikely to result in these sorts of serious physical withdrawal symptoms.

If you eat a lot of sugar, you may crave it. You might like chocolate so much that you think of yourself as a chocoholic. Some research does suggest that similar areas of the brain are working when a person eats a food they crave and when a person uses a drug. But this doesn't mean that "addiction" to food is the same thing as addiction to a drug. It's typically easier to change an eating habit than it is to change a drug habit, for example. As we've discussed in Chapter 7 and elsewhere in this chapter, habits can be persistent, but food also has a nourishing and important role in sustaining our health. The same cannot be said of other truly addictive substances.

EXPERT ADVICE

Professor Stuart Murray, PhD, *University of Southern California, USA*

"Eating disorders are among the most **stigmatized**, lethal, and burdensome of all psychiatric disorders. Imagine a disorder beyond your control, which could literally kill you, which society says is your fault, and where treatment options are limited. We need to do more for all people—boys, girls, men, women—who experience eating disorders."

FASTING, BINGING, AND EVERYTHING IN BETWEEN

You've probably heard about **eating disorders** from the **media** or in a health class at school, but you may not have known that there are several different kinds of eating disorder, or realized that eating disorders can be *really* serious. In fact, they're the most deadly form of mental illness (aside from opioid addiction). It's also likely that most of the information you're familiar with concerning eating disorders relates to girls and women. However, recent research indicates that 75% of all boys report wishing that their body size was different than it currently is. This is not the same thing as having an eating disorder, but it does suggest that, in general, boys would like to look different than they do and are vulnerable to eating disorders.

We'll review the most common eating disorders below. As you read, it is important to understand that the symptoms described can apply to boys, girls, and people with any gender identity, and that anyone who experiences these symptoms should get professional help.

ANOREXIA NERVOSA

Anorexia nervosa, usually referred to as anorexia, is an eating disorder that's relatively rare, but extremely serious. Individuals who develop anorexia typically eat very little and often eat only certain types of foods. They may exercise excessively and tend to be obsessed with food, calories, and other qualities of foods, such as how much fat is in different types of foods. Anorexic patients often avoid social gatherings that include food and may prepare food for others that they don't eat themselves. Anorexic patients are usually concerned with trying to lose weight or stay lean, weigh themselves often, and tend to experience extreme body image concerns. Many individuals with anorexia are underweight, but some are not; you can't always determine who has an eating disorder by looking at them.

The health consequences of anorexia can be very serious. When the body doesn't get enough of the nutrients it needs, a variety of problems may develop. Some of the many health concerns that can develop include dramatic weight loss, stomach pain, weakness, lowered immune functioning (the body's ability to fight illness is reduced), slowed heart rate, overall feelings of coldness and difficulty with temperature regulation, difficulty sleeping, dizziness and fainting, difficulty concentrating, and even death. Caleb's story reminds us that eating disorders can happen to anyone and can be very dangerous.

MY STORY

CALEB WADE, 19 YEARS OLD

I always thought that anorexia was a girls' disorder. I didn't think that it was something that could happen to me.

I didn't grow up worried about my weight. I was tall and pretty thin. But when my heart was broken at the end of 10th grade, a switch was flipped. I was suddenly worried about how others perceived me in a way that I hadn't been before. I coped with this concern and my heartache by going to the gym—a lot. I also started to pay more attention to what I was eating. At the time, I thought that I was just focusing on my health.

It didn't take long before all that exercise and my "healthy" eating resulted in notable weight loss. I also found myself becoming obsessed with food. I was always thinking about what I was eating—and not eating—next. It was around this time that I started seeing a therapist.

One of the primary goals of therapy was weight gain. I knew that my parents and my therapist were all trying to help me, but it didn't work. I kept losing weight until I ended up in the hospital—actually, more than once.

Fortunately, I'm one of the lucky ones, and a few things have made my ongoing recovery possible. My earlier treatment for **obsessive-compulsive disorder (OCD)** has made me more in touch with my thoughts and emotions. Eating-disorder treatment helped me to identify when my thoughts were disordered and ways to change my behaviors. Family-based therapy and having my parents really involved in my recovery was difficult, but essential. Putting on weight and getting healthier helped me think more clearly, and my disordered thoughts became less frequent.

Perhaps the most critical part of my recovery has been the realization that I'm fighting a war to save myself. I spent a lot of energy in high school feeling bad about myself, but at some point that switched to feeling mad at this disorder for taking over my life. There's a lot I want to do in the future, and I'm in college now studying to make it happen. I have to take care of myself if I'm going to make a difference in the world.

I understand that people with anorexia often skip meals or eat very small meals, and that anorexia is a very dangerous disorder. But I've also read about people who use "intermittent fasting" for weight loss, which seems similar to skipping meals. What's the difference? And does intermittent fasting work?

Intermittent fasting has received attention in recent years as an approach to weight loss. It typically involves people eating as they regularly do for 5 days a week and then eating relatively little for a couple of days a week. Some people only eat within a select window of time each day—for example, between 10 a.m. and 5 p.m. The general idea isn't necessarily to limit the amount of food eaten, but to limit what is eaten to certain periods of time.

Research by nutritionists suggests that intermittent fasting can help people lose weight, but not any better than just changing the foods people eat (for example, snacking on fruit instead of unhealthy snacks) or exercising more often. A recent study found that intermittent fasting led to hardly any weight loss—and the weight that was lost was muscle. One of the biggest problems with intermittent fasting is that it leaves people hungry. It's a way of eating that can be difficult for people to stick to long term. In other words, even if it helps people lose weight, they lose muscle, not fat, and they eventually gain weight back over time.

How is intermittent fasting different from an eating disorder? This is a good and complicated question. If someone is intermittently fasting because he is worried about his weight, avoids social situations so that it's easier to avoid food, feels concerned about his body size or shape, and has lost a lot of weight recently, then it's likely that this person has taken fasting way too far and has developed an eating disorder. If someone sometimes skips breakfast, but otherwise eats regularly, that's probably not an eating disorder.

Continued ...

Because intermittent fasting and eating disorders share some similar characteristics, we do not recommend that a child or an adolescent try this approach to weight loss. In fact, this could be especially bad for young people who are still growing and experiencing puberty, because they need a variety of nutrients over the course of the day to stay healthy. We don't recommend this approach to adults, either, because of the similarities between intermittent fasting and disordered eating.

BULIMIA NERVOSA

Bulimia nervosa, or "bulimia," typically involves binging and then purging food. When someone binges, they eat much more than is typical in one sitting. You may feel really full if you eat three or four pieces of pizza, but a real binge would mean eating an entire pizza plus more, in most cases. People with bulimia tend to feel a loss of control and an inability to stop eating when they binge. Sometimes, binges are referred to as a "cheat meal"—a big meal after days or weeks of limited eating (sometimes called "cutting," discussed further below). After a binge, a bulimic person often feels guilty and then engages in some sort of purge. Purging can take different forms, including using medication that leads to vomiting or diarrhea. Sometimes bulimic individuals exercise extensively. The rapper Eminem claims that he developed a form of bulimia by exercising for hours every day. Although it isn't typical to hear a lot about men—especially celebrities—who experience eating disorders, plenty of men have suffered from these problems.

The health consequences of bulimia are somewhat similar to the consequences of anorexia. In both disorders, people are unlikely to get the nutrients they need. Furthermore, for both anorexic and bulimic people, the time and energy focused on food and weight is a major distraction from the rest of their lives. But unlike those with anorexia, bulimic people often develop problems with their stomachs and digestive systems as a result of binging and purging. They may also have difficulty sleeping, difficulty concentrating, problems fighting infection, and muscle weakness. Purging may result in other health concerns, including dental problems and very serious issues including chemical imbalances. These sorts of imbalances can lead to serious complications including death, often without any warning.

BINGE EATING DISORDER

Binge eating disorder (BED) is thought to be the most common eating disorder. People with BED tend to binge (at least once a week for at least 3 months) without purging. Binges are described as excessive in terms of how much is eaten, and they're experienced as uncontrollable. Binging may occur as a means of coping with emotional experiences and typically occur alone. When people binge, they often describe the experience as if they're in a trance. They eat quickly and until they're uncomfortable, and then feel guilty and ashamed afterwards.

People with BED often experience problems with their stomachs and digestive systems. They may get cramps, constipation, heartburn, or other symptoms as a result of their problematic eating habits. They often spend a lot of time and energy thinking about food and what they will eat. People with BED are likely to gain weight, and may experience stigma and shame as a result of their body size.

OTHER SPECIFIED FEEDING OR EATING DISORDERS

Sometimes people have unhealthy eating habits that are not as severe or as consistent as would be required to be diagnosed with anorexia, bulimia, or BED, but their eating habits still disrupt their life. Their habits may lead to drastic weight gain or weight loss. Most importantly, these people are stressed out about their eating, body image, or weight (or all three). These individuals are often diagnosed with having an **other specified feeding or eating disorder**. This long name is really just a way of saying someone has an "other eating disorder."

To receive an official diagnosis of anorexia, for example, patients must have a number of specific symptoms. A patient may fall just short of the required number of symptoms, but he or she may clearly have serious concerns and unhealthy **behaviors** surrounding food. This patient would likely get diagnosed as having an other specified feeding or eating disorder. This diagnosis helps different healthcare providers to realize the seriousness of the patient's symptoms and can help organize treatment for the patient.

MYTHS & MISBELIEFS

> You can never eat *too* healthily.

Eating healthy foods is a good way to take care of your body. However, it is possible to become too concerned with healthy eating. If you find yourself spending a lot of time thinking about what you are eating and feel guilty if you eat anything that is remotely unhealthy, you may have what is referred to sometimes as orthorexia. The American Psychological Association does not recognize orthorexia as a clinical disorder, but it is a term used to describe an overconcern with eating healthy foods, avoiding unhealthy foods, and being rigid about food choice, and often includes body image concerns. People with orthorexia often experience anxiety and obsessive-compulsive tendencies. Although you may benefit physically from eating nutritious foods, taken to the extreme this can become problematic psychologically. Food should be enjoyed! Every meal does not need to include avocado, kale, and almonds.

BODY DYSMORPHIC DISORDER

Body dysmorphic disorder (BDD) is not an eating disorder, but often co-occurs with eating disorders. In other words, people who have eating disorders sometimes have BDD, but just having BDD is not an eating disorder. BDD is also more common among people who have obsessive-compulsive disorder (an anxiety disorder).

BDD is a body image disorder. People with BDD are preoccupied with their bodies' defects and flaws. They are compulsive about tending to their appearance and may go to extremes to alter their appearance, such as obtaining extensive cosmetic surgery. At the heart of BDD is the inability to see oneself as others do and being extremely critical of one's body. People with BDD are preoccupied with their perceived defects and flaws, but are also often anxious and depressed as a result of their preoccupation.

MUSCLE DYSMORPHIA

Muscle dysmorphia is sometimes referred to as the "male eating disorder" or "bigorexia." It is actually a subtype of BDD and more of a body image disorder than an eating disorder. Because the stereotypical ideal male body is muscular, boys and men often focus on increasing their muscularity and lowering their body fat.

In order to become more muscular, boys and men may adopt extreme eating and exercise behaviors and may even use performance-enhancing drugs, such as anabolic steroids. "Bulking" and "cutting" (also discussed in Chapter 5) are discussed in popular publications, on web pages, and in YouTube videos, and are typically used to describe unhealthy efforts to gain muscle by lifting heavy weights for an excessive amount of time and then restricting foods eaten to lose weight. According to recent research, these extreme behaviors may be more common than people realize, with up to 60% of boys adopting unhealthy habits to increase the size of their muscles. Just because these behaviors have become common does not mean that they are a good idea. In fact, people who suffer from muscle dysmorphia tend to think obsessively about their muscles and never feel like they are muscular enough. Even after investing a lot of time in trying to change their bodies, they are not happy with their appearance. Recovering from these obsessive thoughts and compulsive behaviors often requires treatment, just like any other eating or body image disorder. Matt's story reminds us how eating disorders can begin with a focus on athleticism and muscularity.

MY STORY

MATT ROBERT, 23 YEARS OLD

When I was younger, I never saw myself as having body image issues. Looking back now, I can see that I was very aware of how I looked—probably much more than some of my peers (or maybe they were just better at hiding it). When I was about 14, those body image issues really made their feelings known. I think I had been struggling with an eating disorder for 3 years by then, and I was just trying to come out of a really dark time. I took to training and getting back to playing sport again.

Sport ("sports" in the USA, I guess) has always been a massive part of my life, but in my teens I was really striving for the impossible. By age 16, I was playing at a semi-professional level, and this is when the issues took hold in a much bigger way. Being quite a naturally narrow build, I was looking around at my teammates, who were all building muscle and looking bigger, and I felt left out. This was only made worse by the constant comments on my (lack of) size. I felt inadequate and constantly tried to get to something that my body just naturally could not do. This made me end up really unwell and to be honest I am lucky that I am still alive today.

One message I would give to all boys and young men is that it is OK to look how you do. We are all different, and that is not only normal, but beautiful.

Continued ...

We are not robots; we are human beings. What is so much more important is how you feel, your happiness, and finding your way in life. Our bodies will change naturally over time and that is OK. Don't be ashamed to be who you are.

Finally, if you are struggling with your body image, with food, or with your relationship with activity, please seek support for this. Happiness does not come from trying to achieve impossible body image standards, it comes from within. Show yourself some love and **compassion** and strive for whatever makes you truly happy and fulfilled in life. It is not a weakness to struggle—we all do. Admitting that is actually a real strength. We still face so much stigma today being boys/men and struggling with our mental health. It is totally normal to struggle, and by being open, honest, and truthful with yourself and others, you are much more likely to come out on the other side happier, healthier, and with a new passion for life. You might also help someone else.

HOW DOES A PERSON DEVELOP AN EATING DISORDER?

Like any mental health problem, no one *wants* to develop an eating disorder. A person might have concerns about their body image or weight, but this doesn't mean that they want to develop a serious illness. It's important to keep this in mind if a friend or someone you know has an eating disorder (see the Q & A on the next page).

There are many reasons why someone might develop an eating disorder. Usually, people who develop eating disorders are concerned about their weight and don't feel good about their bodies. Sometimes they're overweight, but more often they're not overweight, but are still worried about what they eat and how they look. It turns out that usually a person's

Q+A

Can short-term use of steroids
be enough to help me increase
the size of my muscles without
jeopardizing my health?

Performance-enhancing substances include (illegal) drugs such as anabolic steroids and other legal supplements such as creatine. Pre-workout, muscle-building, and weight-loss supplements often contain a variety of stimulants (a sort of drug) that may increase energy, but place health at risk—even with one use. A recent study found that muscle-building supplements present risk of medical complications that may result in emergency room visits, hospitalization, and even death. The US Food and Drug Association (FDA) found cases of serious liver injury caused by workout supplements. In fact, workout supplements can avoid FDA regulations (that something like ibuprofen or Tylenol would require). Supplements can claim to use a "proprietary blend," meaning they don't have to release the actual amounts of the substances you are consuming. Regulation of these products is much more careful in some other countries, including the UK.

Some research suggests that young men who use muscle-building supplements are more likely to try illegally obtained steroids too. Steroids are prescription drugs for a reason; they pose a variety of serious health risks, especially among young people. Steroids can affect hormones that are important for development, learning, and emotions. For example, steroid use has been linked with a difficulty concentrating, aggression, and anxiety. Sometimes these behaviors and emotions return to normal after steroid use is stopped, but sometimes they do not. In other words, any use of steroids (not prescribed by a doctor—there are some medical uses!) may result in long-term negative behavior and health consequences.

The safest way to build muscle is to focus on a moderate amount of weightlifting (be sure you know what you are doing and don't overdo it!), eat well, and sleep enough. Additional protein and carbohydrate intake can help, but most boys get plenty of protein without thinking about it (see Chapter 6 for more information about protein).

actual weight is much less relevant than is a person's *feelings* about their weight in the development of eating disorders.

Many people who develop eating disorders live in families that talk a lot about food and dieting, or in which others have eating-disorder symptoms themselves. Sometimes family members may tease and make a person feel bad about their food choices or weight.

Media influences are also relevant to individuals' development of eating disorders. As discussed in earlier chapters (see Chapter 4), images of what the "ideal man" looks like feature slender but muscular men. Messages that equate muscularity and lean muscle with masculinity are everywhere in Western cultures. It's easy for people to believe that they'll be happiest if they look a certain way, and to be willing to take drastic measures to achieve that look. The problem is that there are so many serious health problems associated with not maintaining healthy habits. An eating disorder may contribute to weight loss or gain, but will cause many other problems.

Some research suggests that people with certain personalities may be more vulnerable to developing eating disorders. People who are perfectionists or anxious are more likely to worry about things like fitting in with their peers and looking a certain way. This may lead them to be more at risk for an eating disorder. All the factors that may lead to an eating disorder are likely influenced by our biology; some people possess biological characteristics that place them at risk. These are complex disorders,

EXPERT ADVICE

Dr. Jason Nagata, MD, MSc, *University of California, San Francisco, USA*

"An eating disorder may develop when a boy becomes preoccupied with his appearance, body size, weight, food, or exercise in a way that worsens his quality of life. Eating disorders can affect boys of all races, ethnicities, sexual orientations, body shapes, and weights. Eating disorders in boys can lead to serious medical consequences that can affect every organ system in the body. Eating disorders in boys are more likely to get overlooked or diagnosed later than in girls. Boys with eating disorders may pursue a body ideal that is big and muscular. Boys with eating disorders may engage in muscle-enhancing behaviors such as excessive exercise and use of performance-enhancing substances."

and they're very serious. Regardless of the reasons behind a person developing an eating disorder, it isn't their fault that they're sick.

People suffering from an eating disorder usually require treatment by several healthcare professionals including physicians, psychologists, and nutritionists. Unfortunately, because boys and men are not expected to have eating disorders as often as girls and women, they don't always get the treatment they need. If you or someone you know needs body-image or eating-disorder treatment, you may need to talk to more than one doctor to get that help. Waiting is not the answer; early treatment is often more effective than waiting to see if a person grows out of an eating disorder. It's always safer to provide too much help and support to a person than not enough.

I have a good friend who I think has an eating disorder. He's constantly at the gym (for hours every day). He also is really inconsistent in how he eats. Some days he seems to eat hardly anything and some days he eats a lot. I don't want to offend him or seem nosey by asking him if he's OK. What should I do?

It's likely that at some point in your life you'll know at least one person who has an eating disorder. It's important to think about how best to be helpful in these situations. First of all, you probably want to choose whether or not you want to talk to your friend directly, or talk to an adult who may be able to help. It may make sense to do both. If you aren't comfortable approaching your friend directly, you could talk to your parents, one of his parents, or a psychologist, counselor, or teacher at your school. Sharing your concern with a caring adult can help to ease your worry and allow someone else to step in and help.

If you decide to talk with your friend directly, be careful not to blame him for having a problem. No one wants to develop an eating disorder; he has an illness similar to other kinds of physical illnesses. It's often helpful to try to have a calm conversation that allows you to express your concern and worry about him. You could say, "I've noticed that you're spending a lot of time in the gym. I appreciate that you want to look good, but I'm worried that you are overdoing it. I know that, for guys, eating disorders are often all about exercise." It is very possible that your friend does not think of his behaviors as contributing to an eating disorder, so he may react with surprise.

You can direct your friend to some helpful resources online, such as the National Eating Disorders Association eating disorders screening tool (www.nationaleatingdisorders.org/screening-tool). You may want to let him know that you're aware that eating disorders can be very serious—even deadly—and that you care about him getting better and enjoying food and a healthy future. Consider helping him find a way to get professional help. It can be scary for people to ask for help, even though it's probably a good idea for him to talk with his doctor

Continued ...

and a psychologist. At the very least, he could call the National Eating Disorders Helpline (USA 1-800-931-2237) or the Beat Eating Disorders Helpline (UK 0808 801 0677) or use a chatbot developed by psychologists and The Butterfly Foundation (Australia's eating disorders help organization; go to https://butterfly.org.au/chattokit/).

Sometimes people who need medical help aren't ready to get it. It's possible that you could talk with your friend and he may not follow your advice at all. Try not to take this personally, but continue to express your concern to your friend. Most importantly, don't ever shame someone or make them feel bad for having a problem. This is unlikely to help and may only damage your relationship with them.

YOU HAVEN'T BEEN EATING ENOUGH NUTRITIOUS FOOD AND YOU WANT TO DO BETTER

Even if you're certain that you don't have anything resembling an eating disorder, you may find yourself wanting to improve your eating habits as you read this book. As far as health habits go, we're all works in progress. Most of us could improve our eating and activity habits at least a little bit. There are so many food temptations that can pull us off the path of healthy eating: vending machines, drive-throughs, and even options available in the cafeteria at school. Because what we eat has a significant impact on our health, it can be a good decision to work on improving our eating habits. Where should you start?

It's difficult to change any sort of habit, including what you eat. In Chapter 7, we discussed some good ways to work on eating more nutritious foods. One of the most important steps is to work with your current life to make lasting changes. Think about the ways that your surroundings—your family, school, and friends—influence what you eat. If you feel like you could alter a habit at home, maybe eating healthier breakfasts, then talk with your family about how to do this together. If you're always tempted to make a poor choice in the cafeteria at school, you could make a pact with a friend to try to choose water instead of soda. If you and your friends always go out for pizza when you hang out, you may want to suggest other options once in a while.

For some people, improving eating habits may mean eating different types of things, like more vegetables and less fried food. For others, it may mean eating *more* food. It can be difficult to eat intuitively, or to eat when you're hungry and stop when you're full, but this is a valuable approach to think about and practice for the rest of your life. Many experts believe that although it's worth being thoughtful about our food choices, it's even more important to not worry about food and eating. Most—although not all—of us in the USA and Europe are lucky enough to have enough food to keep us alive, and this is what's most important. Food is the fuel that keeps our bodies working. It's good to give our body nutritious fuel, but there is nothing wrong with enjoying all sorts of foods, including less nutritious foods.

HOW YOU EAT IS RELATED TO HOW YOU FEEL

How you eat—even how you think about food—has a big impact on many areas of your life. Part of the connection between how you eat and how you feel is physical; both your brain and your body react to what you eat (or don't eat). If you aren't eating enough and you're hungry, you're also more likely to be tired, unable to concentrate, and maybe even **hangry** (hungry + angry). If you're not eating

MYTHS & MISBELIEFS

Dietary supplements are "all natural," and are the healthiest way to improve how you look, feel, and treat a variety of illnesses such as eating disorders.

You'll notice that we discuss dietary supplements in a few places throughout this book, because they are a source of great confusion among the general public. They are very popular, but very poorly understood by most people. In the USA alone, about $35 billion is spent on vitamins, minerals and other supplements each year. One study found that almost 40% of high-school boys report using protein powder or shakes at some point.

Scientific research suggests that most dietary supplements, including vitamins, minerals, and the other products you may see near them in a health food store or pharmacy (for example, protein powder) do nothing to improve health or treat any illnesses. Furthermore, supplement companies do not have to prove that their products are safe before they begin to sell them in the USA (the UK monitors these products for safety more than the USA). Although supplements are advertised as safe and "natural," it is actually likely that most supplements may do more harm to your health than good.

Dietary supplements should not be taken by boys looking to improve their health or treat any sort of illness. Your health will benefit more from eating vegetables or lean sources of protein than from taking some sort of powder or pill.

nutritious foods, you may also find yourself feeling a lack of energy, being easily distracted, and finding it difficult to learn. Poor nutrition is also associated with an inability to fight off illness and infection, which is part of why people in poor, developing countries are more likely to struggle with health problems not found in wealthier countries.

Your eating habits are also likely to affect how you feel about yourself and your psychological health, even if you never have anything resembling an eating disorder. For example, in one recent study, researchers found that lower self-esteem is associated with poorer eating habits. This may mean that people with low self-esteem don't eat as many nutritious foods, or it may mean that eating nutritious foods seems to have a positive impact on people's self-esteem. Most likely, both of these things are partly true.

In related research, a link has been found between self-compassion, eating behaviors, and body image. What is **self-compassion**? Well, if you're compassionate, you're concerned about others and you show them sympathy. Self-compassion is treating yourself with this same sort of concern and sympathy. People who think of themselves with kindness and caring are more likely to have more intuitive and healthy eating habits than people who think poorly of themselves. Self-compassion is also linked with a **positive body image**. This is just one more reason to treat yourself like you would a good friend.

EXPERT ADVICE

Professor Zali Yager, PhD, *body image researcher, Australia*

"Muscle-building supplements and powders are really quite dangerous for teenage boys; the formulas have not been tested in order to ensure that they are safe for boys who are still growing and developing, or that they will be effective. We tend to see that boys who start to use these products end up feeling worse about themselves and their bodies over time instead of better."

Summing Up #KeepFoodFun

☑ Healthy eating habits include choosing mostly nutritious food options from what is available to you (for example, fruits and vegetables), but also include enjoying food and making eating a fun part of your life.

☑ Always denying yourself foods that you enjoy, or eating too much or too little to feel good, isn't healthy and may lead to disordered eating, or even a serious eating disorder. If you think that you or someone you know may have an eating disorder, talk with an adult and look for treatment as soon as possible.

☑ It's OK to think about improving your eating habits by including more nutritious choices into what you usually eat. But it's not OK to worry about what you eat!

Find out more

• If you have questions about eating disorders, spend some time on the National Eating Disorders and the Beat Eating Disorders' web pages: www.nationaleatingdisorders.org and www.beateatingdisorders.org.uk.

• For more information about dietary supplements and the research that indicates which ones may be helpful versus which ones are *not* supported by scientific research, see the National Institutes of Health's web page: https://ods.od.nih.gov/factsheets/list-all/.

• To read more about the risks associated with steroid use, especially among teens, go to: www.drugabuse.gov/publications/research-reports/steroids-other-appearance-performance-enhancing-drugs-apeds/what-are-risks-anabolic-steroid-use-in-teens.

• Learn more about self-compassion by reading Dr. Kristin Neff's web page: https://self-compassion.org/.

• For more scholarly articles and web pages with information about eating disorders and nutrition, see the companion website for this book: www.TheBodyImageBookforBoys.com.

CHAPTER NINE

BUILDING THE BEST YOU

#ProHealth

> "THE ONLY PERSON YOU ARE DESTINED TO BECOME IS THE PERSON YOU DECIDED TO BE."
>
> Ralph Waldo Emerson

Nurturing a positive body image isn't only about feeling good about your appearance. It's about taking care of yourself—both your body and your mind. In this chapter, we discuss strategies for taking care of yourself that you may want to adopt. We'll also review some things that may interfere with your ability to take good care of yourself so that you can combat them and stay healthy for the rest of your life.

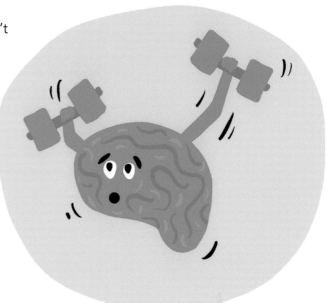

In this chapter you'll learn

○ how to be aware of your physical and mental needs and to aim for positive **embodiment**,

○ how to identify when you may need extra help, such as if you experience anxiety, depression, or a chronic health condition, and

○ the importance of nurturing positive relationships with others who will support you on your journey to a positive body image.

SELF-CARE IS FOR GUYS, TOO

When you hear the term "**self-care**," you may imagine a girly scene complete with a bubble bath and nail polish. However, self-care is for guys and it doesn't have to involve bubble baths (unless you want it to, and it is absolutely OK if you do). Self-care refers to any efforts you make to care for yourself. Sometimes taking care of yourself may even mean that you decide not to do something that you have been asked to do and that you feel is not in your best interests. Taking care of yourself often means asking others for help. Self-care is one of the most important jobs you have.

MANLY FEELINGS

It is extremely unfortunate that there are negative assumptions when it comes to boys and men taking care of themselves—and even acknowledging when they don't feel well (mentally or physically). The cultural messages you may be familiar with suggest that it is "manly" to "tough it out" and it is never acceptable to be upset, sad, hurt, emotional, or ill. This is all ridiculous, of course; you are a person and not a robot!

Some recent research suggests that parents (especially mothers) may expect their daughters to express their emotions, but may not expect the same

of their sons. These beliefs influence how they parent and how comfortable their children end up being expressing their emotions. If you feel you should keep your thoughts, feelings, or emotions to yourself, it is likely that you have been raised to think this way. People around you and the media may have led you to believe that you should keep to yourself! However, feeling isolated and believing it is not possible to talk with others about issues that are important to you may lead to loneliness.

When boys and men feel completely unable to express their emotions they may end up experiencing depression (which we discuss later in this chapter). They also may find themselves engaging in toxic masculinity. Toxic masculinity is a term that has become popular in recent years and is used to describe a strict following of male gender roles. This can be reflected in men behaving as if they don't care about relationships with others and seeking to dominate people in their lives (in other words, they are "in charge of" others, especially women). Toxic masculinity leads boys and men to put others down—not just women, but any men who are not "tough guys." This may include guys who have had different experiences, come from different places, or have different sexual preferences. Seeking to dominate or bully others is unhealthy. It is better to be comfortable with yourself and respect others. To take care of yourself, you must pay attention to your needs, but also be attentive to the needs and desires of others, so that you can maintain healthy relationships.

EXPERT ADVICE

Ed Frauenheim, co-author of *Reinventing Masculinity: The Liberating Power of Compassion and Connection*, USA

"For thousands of years, boys have gotten the message that feelings are for sissies. That boys don't cry. Not only are tears of sadness shameful, but so are tears of joy. The real shame is that we've stunted boys' mental health. Thankfully, an emerging 'liberating masculinity' is freeing boys and men from that emotional straitjacket and giving them permission to feel the full range of human emotions."

WHAT IS MINDFULNESS?

One way to care for yourself is to be mindful of your physical, psychological, social, and emotional needs. Mindfulness actually has two related definitions. To be mindful means to be aware. It's important to spend some time thinking about your needs; for example, you may find that you value some time alone each day. Or maybe you realize that you feel better when you get at least 8 hours of sleep each night.

Mindfulness also refers to being present in the moment, accepting your thoughts and feelings, and paying attention to your thoughts. There are different ways to try to achieve this sort of mindfulness. Some people take deep breaths and try to relax, while others practice yoga or meditate. Meditation techniques aim to train the mind, just as physical activity aims to train the body. Whereas physical activity is all about being active, meditation is about training the mind to be calm.

What does this have to do with body image? For some people, meditation can help them feel calmer and more in touch with their bodies. This sense of "being in touch with" or "happily living in" our bodies is sometimes referred to as embodiment. This may seem obvious, but we *are* our bodies. We cannot escape them. Feeling comfortable and accepting of our bodies is an important part of developing a positive body image.

Some forms of meditation involve stillness and focusing attention on a particular object while trying to clear thoughts from the mind. Meditation can also focus on acknowledging thoughts or concerns and working on accepting them or distancing yourself from them. Meditation includes listening to music that's enjoyable and soothing, and can even include reading or writing/journaling. The goal of any sort of meditation is to feel calm, relaxed, and "centered."

Some people enjoy meditation, but not everyone. You can get better at it with practice, but it may not be for you. It typically involves stillness, reflection, and calmness. Some people don't like to be still, aren't particularly patient at reflecting on their experiences, and are naturally high energy. These people may grow to like meditation, but it also may not be a good fit for them. There are other ways to nurture your physical and emotional selves, so don't worry if meditation doesn't seem to be for you. Sometimes a couple of deep breaths or quick 5-minute breaks can help keep you feeling relaxed and focused.

OTHER WAYS TO RELAX

Typical mindfulness techniques are not for everyone. We've already discussed exercise in detail in Chapter 5, but exercise can be a great way to relax and to support your psychological health. Of course, you have to be doing some sort of exercise that you enjoy in order for it to relax you. Even going on a short run or walk, enjoying the scenery around you, and taking a break from the rest of your day can be a good way to de-stress.

Relaxation practices are often described as solitary activities that you must do alone. We don't think this is necessarily true. If we go to a ballgame with our friends and spend a few hours with our buddies ignoring the stressors in our lives and enjoying each other's company, we are likely to feel relaxed afterwards. In other words, socializing can be a way to relax, and often people we're close to can offer support and advice that makes us feel calmer and less frazzled by the demands of our lives.

There are a million ways to take care of yourself. You might try to think of the ways that you take care of yourself—bathing, brushing your teeth, exercising, seeing your friends—and ask yourself if you should do more of one activity, or perhaps add some self-care activities that you aren't doing at all.

WHAT IF YOU FEEL LIKE YOU NEED EXTRA HELP TO BE YOUR BEST?

There are a lot of great things about growing up, but there are also things that may feel challenging. The changes you experience physically as a result of puberty may feel strange and unsettling. Changes in your social world as you start a different school, participate in new activities, or make new friends can be exciting, but also stressful. Perhaps in part because of these changes, adolescence is a time period in which some mental health disorders tend to emerge (in other words, people may have a biological tendency to experience these disorders that doesn't become obvious until adolescence). Relatively common mental disorders that you may experience in adolescence are depression, anxiety, and substance use disorders. Fortunately, all of these disorders are treatable, and there is a lot you can do to feel better if you experience any of these.

It is really important that you do not ignore signs of depression, anxiety, or substance use disorders if you think you're experiencing any of these. As we discussed earlier in this chapter, boys and men often don't feel comfortable asking for help. This may lead to problems getting bigger and may make treatment more difficult. At the extreme, boys and men may attempt suicide; men are 3.5 times more likely to die by suicide than women.

DEPRESSION

Depression is the most common psychological disorder. We all feel sad sometimes, but depression is more than just sadness. Usually, when a person experiences depression, he experiences physical, cognitive, and emotional symptoms. Physical symptoms may include feeling tired all the time or being unable to sleep, extreme hunger or a lack of appetite, and changes in weight. Sometimes symptoms are more physical and may include headaches and nausea, or irritability or moodiness. Depression may lead a person to have a difficult time concentrating or completing tasks. Depression is often revealed in feelings of worthlessness and despair, as if life is not worth living.

Depression can be mild and last for a few months, or it may be severe and last for years. Sometimes depression comes and goes across a person's life. Life experiences, such as the loss of a loved one, can lead to depression, but most scientists believe that there is often a biological and genetic component to depression. Regardless of what leads someone to experience depression, it isn't his fault. No one wants to feel sad and hopeless, and anyone who does should consider seeking advice from a doctor or counselor—especially if the symptoms of depression last for more than a few weeks.

There are different treatments for depression, and often a combination of treatments works the best. Talking with a therapist can be an important part of treatment for depression (see Q & A, below). Antidepressant medication can also be helpful, and there are many different types of these medications that work on different brain chemicals. They are not magical pills that change who a person is, but they can be an important part of treatment for depression.

If you think you're depressed, be sure to talk with an adult who you trust about finding treatment. There are steps you can take on your own—talk with friends, exercise, participate in activities you enjoy—that may make you feel better, but don't try to tackle depression on your own.

MYTHS & MISBELIEFS

> Vitamins and other natural supplements are the best and safest way to treat depression.

If you're concerned that you or someone you care about needs treatment for depression, the first step is probably for the depressed person to talk with a therapist. There are no downsides to talking with someone who can offer support, new ways to think about problems that may contribute to depression, and strategies for coping.

There are many types of therapists. Some may offer free services at your school or in a local clinic. Some may see patients in a private practice and charge by the hour. Some therapists are trained to help people cope specifically with depression (versus other mental health issues). Some are trained to help children and adolescents. The goal is to find a therapist

Continued ...

who best fits the needs of the person experiencing a problem in terms of where they provide treatment, what their fees may be, and their ability to help cope with depression in particular.

Some people who experience depression may benefit from antidepressant medications or other similar medications. The most popular of these is probably Prozac, although there are many different kinds of antidepressants (most of which have been created more recently than Prozac). Antidepressant medication can be truly life saving for some people. However, these medications do sometimes come with side effects that are undesirable, such as drowsiness, dry mouth, and even nausea.

Some people prefer not to take medications unless absolutely necessary. They may seek out a different sort of remedy, such as vitamins. While there is not a lot of scientific evidence to suggest that vitamins will help someone cope with depression, according to the Mayo Clinic (a prestigious medical organization in the USA), vitamin B12 and other B vitamins may alter brain chemistry in such a way as to affect mood. Vitamin D has also received some attention as possibly being associated with mood. **St. John's Wort** is a supplement that is often described as helpful to treating depression. However—and this is pretty important—it can interfere with other medications used to treat depression and cause serious side effects and problems. We don't recommend you use St. John's Wort unless you have discussed this option with your healthcare provider.

As discussed throughout this book, vitamins and natural supplements are not regulated by the Food and Drug Administration (FDA) in the USA (although they are regulated in the UK). What does that mean? Well, it means that unlike other medicine, there are no quality checks on what contributes to the creation of vitamins and supplements in the USA, so there may be risks associated with vitamins and supplements. And in the case of vitamin D, most people get what they need just from sunlight.

ANXIETY

Most likely, you have felt anxious at least once in your life. Maybe you've had to give a presentation at school and you felt yourself start to sweat or felt your heart race. This is a normal emotional response to a stressful situation. However, if you feel anxious a lot of the time, then you may have an anxiety disorder. There are different types of anxiety disorders, and all of them tend to affect people's ability to concentrate and focus, and often lead people to avoid certain situations. Anxiety can also affect sleep patterns (for example, making it difficult to sleep) and eating habits (leading people to eat more or less than they usually do). People who have anxiety disorders usually experience symptoms nearly every day for 6 months or more, and have a hard time keeping up with their daily routines at home, work, or school.

Anxiety can be very difficult to deal with, but it's treatable. Talking with a therapist can be a good first step toward coping with anxiety. A therapist can help you think through what's making you anxious and help you change habits and behaviors that may contribute to your anxiety. Anti-anxiety medication may also prove helpful. Similar to antidepressant medication, anti-anxiety medication alters the chemicals in a person's brain and can make a person feel calmer and happier. Stress management techniques, such as yoga and other approaches to mindfulness, can also help to reduce anxiety, but many people need more than this to cope.

SUBSTANCE USE DISORDER

Addiction, or substance use disorders, occur when a person is unable to control their use of legal (for example, alcohol or nicotine—the substance found in cigarettes) or illegal (for example, cocaine) drugs or medication. These are complicated disorders that affect physical and mental health. Substance use disorders may occur for a variety of reasons. For example, a person may experiment with a substance and then become physically addicted to it; or a person may use a drug to cope with stress, perhaps to help him feel relaxed or distracted, and then become addicted. It is also possible that a doctor may prescribe a medication, such as an opioid (pain killer), that leads to addiction. Scientists believe that there are biological and genetic factors that contribute to addiction, with some people being more likely than others to develop substance use disorders. In other words, there are many environmental and personal influences that may contribute to a substance use disorder.

If someone you know experiences a substance use disorder, it's not his fault; he was likely trying to cope as best he could and fell into addiction. No one wants to develop a life-threatening health problem. These problems are incredibly serious. They can lead people to make very poor life choices (for example,

Symptoms of substance use disorders

- A need to use the substance regularly, maybe every day or more than once a day

- Taking more and more of the substance over time

- Thinking about the substance a lot and spending time, money, and energy getting it

- Not being able to do other things that are important to you or your family, like meeting school or work obligations because of your substance use

- Engaging in unsafe behaviors, such as driving or taking care of other people while under the influence of a substance.

- Not being able to stop using the substance without feeling some physical withdrawal, such as nausea, vomiting, shakes, headaches, or body aches

selling possessions so that they can afford the drug) and lose the ability to lead regular lives, maintaining a job and family. Treatment from trained medical professionals, therapists, and even treatment centers are often necessary for a person to recover from an addiction.

I've heard that once someone is an alcoholic, they are always an alcoholic. Is this true?

This is a very good and very complicated question. Any habit or addictive behavior (in other words, a serious habit) is very difficult to change. When it comes to alcohol addiction or any substance use disorder, the habit is not just psychological but also physical. What we mean by that is that an alcoholic's body will adapt to alcohol use and go through withdrawal without the alcohol. An addiction is more than just a bad habit; the body adjusts to the substance in ways that can make it very difficult to stop use.

If an individual stops drinking alcohol (or using any other drug), their body will gradually adjust to this positive change. What happens then? It is typically recommended that the person avoid alcohol permanently. There is always the risk of falling back into addiction if the person drinks alcohol, even in moderation.

Organizations like Alcoholics Anonymous, which offers group therapy and other sources of support for alcoholics, believe that once a person is an alcoholic, they always will be, and abstinence (completely avoiding alcohol) is necessary. However, it is possible that some people will be able to consume alcohol safely at some point after recovering from addiction. It is just difficult to know which people this could be possible for—and who could end up experiencing a life-threatening addiction disorder all over again.

EXPERT ADVICE

Timothy Wenger, *founder, The Man Effect, www.themaneffect.com, USA*

"I wish an older man had told me when I was young that it is common to encounter anxiety, depression, stress, and other hard mental challenges while growing up. Mental challenges are a part of life, and it is completely admirable when men choose to overcome these life challenges. I have personally experienced victory over hardships like this through therapy, talking with close friends, and journaling. I hope young men know that no matter what life throws at them, it's OK to find help if you don't know what to do."

OTHER REASONS FOR EXTRA SELF-CARE

Some people need extra self-care because of a physical health condition or disability. In fact, by adulthood, more than half of all people experience some type of chronic (long-term) health condition. These conditions may be somewhat minor, such as seasonal allergies, or they may be more complicated and serious, such as **diabetes** or **heart disease**. Sometimes mental health and physical health conditions are related; people with chronic health problems are more likely to experience depression, for example. Most chronic conditions require extra self-care in order for people to function optimally.

It can be very difficult to maintain the sort of health **regimen** that may be required if you have (or develop) a chronic condition or disability. Your doctor is likely to prescribe medicine that may be helpful. You may have many doctors' appointments. You may need to make changes to your **lifestyle**, including changes to what you eat or what sort of exercise

BRAD LINCOLN, 15 YEARS OLD

I feel good about my body these days. I've always eaten pretty healthy foods and I have played sports since I was a young kid. Being active has always been a fun way to hang out with friends. Now, I also work out to help me be more competitive in the sports I play. My friends have encouraged me to work out with them. Once my body started changing a little bit, it made me feel good; I'd notice that I looked and felt a little bit more fit than the week before.

I found out that I had type 1 diabetes when I was 7 years old. That has meant a lot of doctors' appointments and much more attention to my diet than the average person requires. In the beginning, I was insecure about being different and having a body that didn't "work" like everyone else's.

Nowadays, I take care of my diabetes on my own more and my parents aren't as involved as they once were. I view my doctors' appointments differently these days, too. I don't think there's any reason to be ashamed of needing extra help from a doctor; most people need some sort of extra help at some point. Over time, I have learned to care less about what other people think about me (and my diabetes) and I feel more confident.

My advice to younger kids is to just be yourself and not think too heavily about what others think or say. If you want to make changes in what you eat or how much you exercise, do so because you want to and not because somebody else wants you to.

you do. In these circumstances, it's normal to feel somewhat let down by your body, or to wish that you didn't have to deal with these things.

In recent research looking at body image among people who experience chronic pain, people who are more accepting of their pain tend to have more positive body images. Health problems don't have to lead people to view their bodies negatively. It really matters how people think about their health. If they're accepting of their health problems—after all, most people will have some kind of health problem at some point—it's less disruptive to their feelings about their body overall. This isn't to say that you should feel glad about having to deal with a health problem, but if you do experience a health problem or disability, there are things you can do to help yourself cope. Never feel like you need to deal with this sort of thing alone. Support from caring others can be important if you find yourself in need of an extra dose of support. There are also psychologists who are trained to help people who are dealing with challenging health issues; they can be a huge help if you find yourself having a tough time.

BROS

There are a lot of unfortunate stereotypes about "real men" being tough and independent, but everyone needs support, help, and love from others. Friends can be an important part of growing up and developing body positivity for a variety of reasons. Feeling good about yourself, body and mind, can be easier when you feel like others feel good about you, too. This isn't to say that you let other people determine your sense of yourself, just that we all find it helpful to feel supported by other people.

Maybe you don't feel like you have a lot of close friends, and that's OK. Or maybe you don't feel like you fit in well at your school, or that other kids

don't share your interests. There are many successful adults who describe themselves as loners during their childhood. Both Bill Gates (the co-founder of Microsoft and one of the wealthiest people in the world) and Steve Jobs (the deceased co-founder of Apple) have been described as "nerds" who didn't fit in with their classmates growing up. Like them, you may find enjoyment in developing a particular skill or hobby, and you may eventually meet more people who share your interests. Even if you don't feel like you have close friends now, this doesn't mean that you won't develop important friendships later, or that you shouldn't try to connect with people you enjoy spending time with.

Your family may be a valuable source of support, especially if you feel that your friendships are lacking in any way. However, it's totally normal for you to prefer the company of friends your own age to parents or other family members. It's also typical for teens to feel like their parents don't understand what their lives are like at school and with kids their age. To a certain extent, this is probably true. But in most cases, your family wants what is best for you, and they want you to grow up to be happy and healthy. Even if it doesn't feel like they "get you," they're usually happy to talk with you and offer whatever support they can. Sometimes you just have to give them a chance.

Some people don't have close family relationships, and for a variety of reasons may not develop a lot of close friendships in their childhood and adolescence. However, there are a lot of other people who care about you and can be a friend to you. Maybe there is a teacher or a coach you admire, and who seems invested in you. It's OK to turn to that person for advice. They probably chose their careers because they enjoy hanging out with kids and want to be helpful to people just like you. There is good evidence that adult mentors (trusted adult advisors) can have very positive effects on young people's lives. When our students have asked us for advice, we always do our best to be helpful and we feel flattered that they want our advice. You're probably not going to burden a teacher, coach, or other adult in your life if you turn to them for advice or support. Remember, they were once kids, too.

YOUR LOVE LIFE

At some point during your adolescence, you're likely to want to form a romantic relationship with a boy or a girl. You'll say that you're "hanging out," or that you "like" or that you're "with" this person. Maybe this relationship will turn serious, maybe it won't. Maybe there will be many of them while you're a teenager, maybe there won't be any until you're an adult. Why are we talking about romance in a book about body image? Because all of our relationships impact us in different ways. Body image isn't just about how we look, but how we feel about ourselves. Our relationships can play a role in all of this.

The start of a romantic relationship of any kind can affect how you think about yourself and may challenge who you are. You may feel like you should try to be someone different to be liked by someone you're interested in, or who is your boy/girlfriend. If you're concerned about your appearance due to your interest in another person, this may be fairly normal. However—and this is important—never feel like you need to look or be someone different to attract someone else's interest. A significant other should be a source of support and love and only add to your positive sense of yourself. In fact, there is research to suggest that people who are in serious relationships typically feel better about their body image than people who are not.

PORN, LOVE, AND SEX (NOT NECESSARILY IN THAT ORDER)

It is normal during your tween and teen years to start to feel attracted to others (girls, boys, or both!) and romantically and sexually curious about others. For many boys, their first explorations of physical and emotional relationships are in television shows or movies they watch. If you find yourself paying closer attention to teenagers in a movie who start

to date or kiss each other, that is to be expected. If you find yourself interested in sex in TV and movies, that is also normal and not something to be embarrassed about.

Many young people watch television shows and movies on a smart phone, tablet, or laptop that is connected to the internet. They also may find "adult" movies—aka **pornography** or porn— on the internet. Adult movies, X-rated movies, or pornography are all movies that contain explicit nudity and sexual interactions. In other words, people are usually completely naked. These movies are usually made by men for

boys and men. In fact, in one recent study, the **majority** of men (over 90%) reported watching pornography in the last 6 months.

Although pornography watching may be common, it has the potential to be very problematic. First of all, most of the people featured in pornography do not look like average people. In particular, their bodies are likely to be more slender, muscular, and hairless than the average person. Men who are porn stars are likely to have larger-than-average pecs and penises, while women who are porn stars are likely to have larger-than-average breasts. Many

porn stars have had cosmetic surgery to look as they do. People you see in pornography are not your role models; trying to look like these people is likely to make you feel inferior and disappointed with your own appearance. Also, avoid holding other people (for example, your romantic partners) to the standards set by porn stars or you are likely to find yourself disappointed.

Pornography also tends to feature sexual encounters in which men act aggressively and women are **portrayed** in submissive roles (at least, this is true of pornography that features heterosexual encounters). Women are often **objectified** or treated like objects, not like people with feelings. Men more often than not take control of the interaction and women go along with men's preferences. Often, pornography features interactions that are violent, not loving or gentle. This is not how most adults expect or hope their sexual encounters to be; people tend to want a loving, positive

experience, and want their partner to have a positive experience. It is important for partners to communicate with each other about their preferences, likes, and dislikes if they are going to have a satisfying intimate relationship.

Pornography usually features sexual encounters that are not a part of romantic or emotional relationships. It is possible to have sex with someone that you do not love (or even care about) and to have sex outside of relationships. However, these types of sexual encounters may lead you to feel objectified. Often, it is viewed as "manly" for men to have sex without becoming emotionally connected with the person they are physically involved with. However, some research suggests that married individuals tend to report having more satisfying sexual relationships than non-married people. Being in a committed, loving relationship can be good for physical connection.

A FINAL THOUGHT ABOUT BUILDING YOUR BEST SELF

Taking good care of yourself and nurturing your body image will take some time and energy. It's OK to think of this as a priority in your life, and you shouldn't feel guilty for spending this time on yourself. You should expect that other people who care about you will support your efforts to develop a positive body image and become the best person you can.

How do you know how to have sex? I mean, I understand the basics, but what if I do something wrong?

Probably everyone worries a little bit about this before they have their first sexual experience. It's not the sort of thing you can really learn about entirely by reading a web page. There is a lot of information about sex and sexuality on the internet. A lot of the information is inaccurate or incomplete. We recommend that you take your questions to a trusted adult or an evidence-based book. Healthy sexual expression is a normal part of life and is not something to be ashamed about.

We hope that your first sexual experience is positive and with someone you care about, and who cares about you. This can make it easier to talk about your physical relationship and be more certain that both you and your partner are comfortable. Of course, if for any reason your first experience is not positive, that does not mean that your future sexual experiences won't be.

It is incredibly important that you are sure that your partner wants to have sex with you. We know that this may seem very basic, but sometimes partners do not communicate about where their physical relationship is heading, and one person ends up feeling (or being) hurt or taken advantage of. It is a really good idea that you know your partner has consented to be sexually intimate with you, and that you have a discussion about the protection you will use to avoid sexually transmitted diseases and unintended pregnancies. When we say "consent," we mean that you have specifically talked with your partner about being sexually involved and you are sure that your partner is comfortable with this. You can't just rely on your perception that your partner is comfortable; **you have to ask and you have to have a discussion. You also have to allow your partner to change his or her mind.**

As we discussed above, our relationships can influence how we feel about ourselves. Having a boyfriend or girlfriend may make you feel attractive, appreciated, or even loved. But don't rely on others to feel those things about yourself. And don't feel like you need to know exactly what you are doing in the bedroom to gain anyone else's approval.

ROBERT HARRISON, 22 YEARS OLD

I was pretty thin growing up, so I didn't have a lot of concerns about my body. I don't think I experienced much scrutiny about my body when I was young, and I was not particularly worried about my weight.

I think my freshman year of college was really a defining time for my body image. At the start of college, I found myself adopting unhealthy eating and sleep habits and I gained a fair amount of weight. When I went back home for the first time, everyone commented on my weight. More than one person called me "fat," and I knew they weren't joking. This caused me to take a hard look at myself (literally, I looked in the mirror!) and I didn't like what I saw. I decided I needed to make changes to my diet and eat more healthily.

What's probably confused my body image and sense of self somewhat is that I have never really conformed to typical gender norms. I can remember buying my first Vogue magazine when I was only 8 years old and flipping through the pages, entranced by the beautiful (and thin!) models. I wanted to be beautiful and glamourous in the ways that both women and men can be. I still find fashion exciting.

I also found that becoming sexually active really affected my body image. When you are intimate with someone else and really let your guard down, you feel very vulnerable. Letting another person see your body can be scary but can also bring you closer to that person. We all want to be loved in spite of any imperfections we see, but it is hard to put that to the test in real life.

If I was to give my younger self advice, I would say to really focus on being healthy and happy. Eat what you like, just be more mindful of portions, and be more active (but you don't have to go to the gym, just do some sort of activity you enjoy). Make changes only for yourself and not to please anyone else. You have to love who you are, regardless of who you are.

Summing Up #ProHealth

☑ Developing your positive body image means taking care of yourself, body and mind. There are many ways to do this—everything from physical activity to hobbies may help you feel good.

☑ If you feel that you need extra support as you care for yourself, talk with a counselor, therapist, doctor, or other adult who can offer that support or find helpful resources. It is brave to admit that you need help to cope with a mental health or physical health concern.

☑ Nurturing your relationships with other people is an important part of taking care of yourself. Be sure to communicate openly with your friends and romantic partners so that you can build emotional intimacy (closeness) with the people you care about.

Find out more

- There is a chapter by Catherine Cook-Cottone about self-care and body image in the book *Body Positive: Understanding and Improving Body Image in Science and Practice* (2018), edited by Elizabeth Daniels, Meghan Gillen and Charlotte Markey. Publisher: Cambridge University Press.

- For information about therapists who may be of help in treating depression or anxiety, see the American Psychological Association's web page (www.apa.org/topics/depression/index) or the British Psychological Society's web page (www.bps.org.uk/).

- For information about substance use disorders and treatment options, check out the National Institute on Drug Abuse (www.drugabuse.gov/) and We are With You in the UK (www.wearewithyou.org.uk)

- Dr. Jennifer Lang has written a book for teens that covers communication, safety, and other important topics you may be curious about, called *Consent: The New Rules of Sex Education* (2018). Publisher: Althea Press.

- For more scholarly articles and web pages with information about mental health and self-care, see the companion website for this book: www.TheBodyImageBookforBoys.com.

CHAPTER TEN

MAKE A DIFFERENCE

#BeTheChange

"ACT AS THOUGH WHAT YOU DO MAKES A DIFFERENCE. IT DOES."

William James, American philosopher and psychologist

When you started to read this book, you may not have been certain that it was really for you. It's likely that you believed that body image was an issue that girls dealt with, not something relevant for boys. Hopefully, you now understand that body image is important for everyone and is much more than just how you feel about your body. Accepting yourself, growing into an adult, and **being you** are important to maintaining both your physical and psychological health.

Taking care of your body, accepting it, and protecting your health are important parts of developing a **positive body image**. Our culture emphasizes the importance of our appearance, making it easy for us to doubt ourselves and experience body dissatisfaction. Hopefully, after reading this far, you understand that you can choose to have a positive body image, even though it may need a bit of work on your part. You and your body are inseparable; your body is the place where you "live" and it is worth spending some time to make that home comfortable and joyful.

Nurturing a positive body image is important not only because your body image affects many other aspects of your mental and physical health, but also because you can contribute to how others think about their bodies. If you think and talk about your body differently from the ways that other people typically do (which, unfortunately, is usually negatively), you can help promote positive change. Or, in the words of William James, you can "make a difference" by acting as though what you do matters—because it does!

It's not always easy to do things differently. In this chapter, we want to leave you with some reminders of why it's important to do so, some potential obstacles on your personal journey, and some ideas to think about when you feel discouraged.

In this chapter you'll learn

○ the importance of being kind and accepting of yourself and others, and not falling for other people's narrow ideas about what is attractive or how you should look,

○ how focusing on meaningful issues outside of yourself can contribute to your positive sense of yourself, and

○ that you can play a part in helping others develop positive body images.

REMEMBER: YOU ARE YOUR OWN WORST CRITIC

We can be harder on ourselves than we ever are on anyone else, and we can get into a cycle. We feel bad about ourselves for not looking a certain way, and then we feel bad for caring that we don't look a certain way. Then we can feel even worse for spending time and energy on these worries.

If you feel down on yourself, take a step back and try to quiet these negative thoughts. Remember the importance of self-compassion and self-acceptance. Both of these attitudes will do a lot more for you than self-hate ever will. No one is perfect by everyone's standards, so you can stop aiming for perfect. Work toward treating yourself with kindness and acceptance.

DON'T COMPARE OR DESPAIR

It's natural for us to compare ourselves to other people, but this tendency to compare ourselves to others, or social comparison, can be problematic. We're all unique in our own ways, and trying to be like someone else will rarely work. Changing our looks (or our personalities, for that matter) is harder than it appears. Most of our qualities have a strong biological component that make them difficult to change. It's best to love yourself as you are.

We can learn from the science examining social comparison. Most recently, researchers have examined how comparing ourselves to others on social media can be a negative experience for many people. One trick you can use is to focus on the emotional message in posts, not the content so much. People who see positive things ("look at how happy he looks") and think about the positive emotions shown ("it's great to see someone looking happy") have a more positive experience using social media. They actual report an improvement in their own mood. The trick is not to take it a step further and think, "He looks so happy and I'm not that happy—what's wrong with me?" Comparing is what leads to despairing, so don't go there.

A lot of kids at my school wear sports jerseys and sweatshirts with team logos on them. I'm not really into sports, but I want to fit in. Is it silly to wear jerseys and sweatshirts from teams I don't really care about so that I don't stand out?

It's important to realize that many people—perhaps, most—care a great deal about fitting in. How we present ourselves to the world, including the clothes we wear, is one of the ways we try to fit in. Most people don't intentionally wear clothes that are different from the current styles, because they want to blend in and seem in touch with current trends. Don't feel bad for wanting to look like other people, or for caring about fitting in.

What's important to realize is that there's no reason that you *have* to wear anything in particular, ever, aside from clothes that cover your body and keep you warm. It's OK to wear clothes that you like or that represent your interests. Having a unique style may be something that people value about you. After all, it'd be boring if everyone wore the same clothes. In fact, when kids wear school uniforms, the whole point is to keep clothing boring and less of a distraction from learning. But most people don't want to wear a uniform outside school.

In addition to seeing kids at school adopt particular styles in terms of their clothes, shoes, hair and possibly even their backpacks and socks, we're all bombarded with so many advertisements for material goods and products that it's easy to feel like there is something wrong with us and that we need to "fix" ourselves by dressing a certain way or using certain products. It can seem like success in life is all about having certain things. Try to remember that clothes and shoes and other things change what we look like but not who we are. It's important, but sometimes very difficult, to keep this in perspective and realize that who we are—what makes us a caring person, a valued friend, and a decent human being—has very little to do with the clothes we wear and other material things.

EXPERT ADVICE

Professor Scott Griffiths, PhD, *University of Melbourne, Australia*

"It is normal and expected that boys care about how they look because our culture compels them to care. The trick is for boys' caring about their appearance to be healthy. The line between healthy and unhealthy appearance investment will be different for everyone, but finding it, blurred and indistinct as it may be, is necessary so that boys can reconcile their thoughts and feelings about their bodies and move forward through life as healthy, balanced individuals."

YOU ARE MORE THAN YOUR APPEARANCE

You are so much more than how you look. Your sense of self and who you are becoming should not be based on your appearance. Your thoughts, behaviors, talents, and relationships with other people should be more central to your self-esteem than your appearance. Remember that advertising is intended to make you focus on your appearance and forget the other important parts of yourself.

The psychologist Renee Engeln describes an overemphasis on appearance at the cost of focusing on more important things—family, education, careers, relationships—as beauty sickness. Most of her work has focused on women, but the same ideas apply to men. There is nothing wrong with the desire to be good-looking. The problem arises when you forget to want to be anything else.

Very attractive people sometimes get more attention from others, something called "pretty privilege" in the media. However, there is a serious downside to being valued for your appearance. For one thing, maintaining your looks often requires a lot of work. It's hard to be engaged with the world and enjoying your life if you're constantly worried about your hair or what clothes you're wearing. You can choose to care less about your looks (and other people's looks as well). You can remember that it's your body that allows you to move, be in, and experience the world. It's what allows you to do so much—it's *not* what's holding you back. Hugo's story reminds us that it can be difficult to feel happy with your appearance, but that it's possible to grow into yourself and become more comfortable with your looks.

HUGO ALONSO, 21 YEARS OLD

I know everyone says you should always love yourself and your imperfections, but it isn't always that simple. Ever since I was little, I was very skinny. My sternum pokes out more than regular people, so I was called things like "bird chest." I don't mind being called names sometimes, but it does affect me when I'm feeling insecure. I guess I'm insecure in general about my body because I feel like I'm too skinny and I'm not the best-looking guy in my opinion. Like every other guy, I wish I was taller, even though I am not exactly short. Recently, one of my friends told me I'm lucky that I'm tall and Puerto Rican, because most Latinos are short.

I think the one thing that has had the most influence on how I see my body is the media. I say this because the media is constantly showing you "the perfect body." Growing up, it was pretty clear that it wasn't mine. But I think it wasn't that much of a concern to me until high school. Once I was in high school, I felt like I wanted girls to notice me more, and I'd have to have a better-looking body for that to happen. Surprise, surprise! All the men on TV and in the media who have girlfriends and are famous are muscular men. It's easy to look around and feel like being more muscular is better.

I wish I had realized when I was growing up that my body was still developing. I was growing and changing and shouldn't have felt so down about my body. I think a lot of people can agree that they don't like something about their bodies, but there is no reason to think that we all have to love everything. Your body is just one part of who you are.

MYTHS & MISBELIEFS

> **People are getting taller and more muscular across time. It's evolution and has nothing to do with what we view as attractive.**

There is a bit of truth to this, because the human body has evolved a great deal across time. Evolution is not responsible, however, for changes in height and body build that are notable in the last century. Evolution takes thousands and thousands of years to leave a noticeable impact on how human beings appear physically.

In most countries around the world, both men and women have grown significantly taller in the last 100 years. For example, the average American man used to be about 5' 7" tall (171 cm). Now, the average American man is closer to 5' 10" tall (177 cm). In Britain, the average man was about 5' 6" tall (168 cm) 100 years ago, but is now also about 5' 10" (177 cm). How tall you end up being has a lot to do with how tall your parents are, but these changes in populations are believed to be due to improvements in nutrition and reductions in childhood infections. A society with healthy and well-nourished kids seems to produce taller people on average.

In terms of our modern-day mania for muscles, this seems to be a cultural creation. Across the 20th century, celebrities, media images, and even children's toys have grown more muscular. For example, researchers have measured action figures from the 1970s and 1980s compared with action figures created in the 2000s. Batman, Superman, GI Joe, The Hulk, and Spiderman all gained a significant amount of muscle across approximately 25 years. When scaled to the dimensions of a typical man, the average of these action figures used to have a chest circumference that was 115 cm, but now they have an average chest circumference of 179 cm.

It's easy to see why boys today would feel like it's more important to be tall and muscular than boys did a generation ago. However, it's really important to keep in mind that your height and body build are not the most important things about you.

DON'T STIGMATIZE

A big problem with the cultural focus on our appearance is that it's usually all about one (or a few) particular look(s). It's rarely about diversity and inclusion—accepting everyone as they are. Few people can fit into the exact "looks" deemed attractive by our culture, because we all come in different shapes and sizes. Most of us aren't tall, broad-shouldered, and most of us don't have a six-pack. We have different colored skin, hair, and eyes. We have different sized noses, ears, and biceps. Defining attractiveness more broadly, to include some of these variations, is an important way to appreciate one another and work toward accepting ourselves.

Unfortunately, there is often far more cultural focus on **stigmatizing** people who don't fit society's views of attractiveness than in accepting people who look different. Stigma is probably a word you've heard before, but maybe you aren't sure exactly what it means. People can be stigmatized because of many qualities: race, gender, disability status, and weight are common sources. If someone is stigmatized, they are mistreated due to these qualities and are often assumed to have negative characteristics associated

with these qualities. **Weight stigma** (also referred to as **weight bias** and **weight-based discrimination**) occurs when a person is mistreated because he is viewed as either overweight or underweight – anything that is not society's idea of the "right" weight. The person is thought to be responsible for his weight and may be assumed to be lazy or addicted to junk food if he has a larger body or to not eat enough if he has a smaller body.

Weight stigma is incredibly problematic, not just because it's unfair to mistreat anyone based on how they look, but also because it's associated with other problems. When a person experiences stigma, they often start to believe others' negative views of them. Experiencing weight stigma has also been associated with the development of body dissatisfaction, eating disorders, and depression. Unfortunately, weight stigmatization has increased in recent years. In fact, some scientists who study weight stigma have referred to it as the last acceptable form of discrimination. What they mean is that people often feel that it's acceptable to mistreat overweight people because it's their fault that they're overweight. Hopefully, after reading this book you understand that weight is a complicated issue, and our size—and our appearance in general—has a lot to do with our biology. Furthermore, blaming or mistreating people for anything is rarely a helpful way to interact with them. Just as self-compassion is incredibly important, compassion for others is essential, too.

EXPERT ADVICE

Professor Jeffrey Hunger, PhD, *Miami University, Ohio, USA*

"Stigma weighs heavily on the health and well-being of larger individuals. We need to take care not to negatively judge, tease, or reject people because of their weight. Instead, we should support and embrace body diversity—doing so can even help us feel better about our own bodies."

COVERING

It's possible that you have not felt stigmatized because of your appearance in general or your weight in particular. It's also possible you've felt the need to hide part of yourself so that you can fit in. A famous **sociologist** (someone who studies people's lives in a social context) named Erving Goffman referred to this desire to cover up part of who you are so that you are perceived favorably as "**covering**." You may find yourself covering when you hold back an emotional response to a movie you are watching with friends—fear or sadness—because you don't want to be seen as "weak." You may find yourself covering when you pretend to be interested in sports, because you want your father to see you as "manly." You may find yourself covering when you wear your hair in a certain (masculine) hairstyle that is popular among your friends (even though you'd rather grow your hair long), because you don't want to be viewed as "girly."

Some qualities that you possess cannot be hidden. In a perfect world, you would never feel a desire to hide anything about who you are. Our desire to fit in can be powerful, however. It isn't wrong to want to fit in and be liked by others. It is also not wrong—in fact we believe it is brave—to be willing to stand out from the crowd, in terms of your appearance, beliefs, or behavior. We also think it is important to consider that most people are likely to find themselves covering at some times. To live completely authentically is an aspiration we have for you, but we also believe it is necessary to be compassionate toward both yourself and others who may not always feel able to do so. The more people express themselves as they really are, the easier it will be for others to be who they truly are.

TRY TO THINK OUTSIDE YOURSELF

Scientists have discovered that focusing on the world outside yourself can be good for how you feel about yourself. In this research, people who engaged with projects or causes that they thought were important, including focusing on schoolwork or volunteering at an animal shelter, spent less energy concerned with their own bodies.

Thinking about issues other than those concerning oneself may improve body image and increase happiness.

It makes sense, right? There are only so many hours in the day, and if you fill those hours with work or causes that are meaningful to you, there will be less time to worry about whether or not you're wearing the most stylish, new brand of tennis shoes. And, you may feel less inclined to care!

Q+A

What's one easy thing we can all do to help improve other guys' body image?

Part of what leads guys to develop body image concerns is feeling that how they look is important and affects how they are judged by others. Our culture sends us all the message that our looks matter in a variety of ways, through advertising, music, movies, and social media. What if we rejected some of these messages and focused more on other things?

Who you are as a boy—and eventually a man—does not depend on your appearance. You can be an amazing teacher when you grow up, but how tall you are will not affect your ability to influence your students. You can be an inspiring doctor one day, but the size of your biceps will not affect how many lives you save. You can be a writer of books that are adored, but your hairstyle will not affect how many people read your words.

You can improve your own and others' body images by spending time and energy on interests that have nothing to do with your appearance. You can think about being you and becoming someone you are proud of. How you live your life will set an example for others, and may influence others to develop similar values.

BE IN TOUCH WITH WHO YOU ARE BECOMING AS A MAN

You have choices about who you become, but you can't choose everything about yourself. Some qualities are beyond your control—if your parents are both tall, you're likely to be tall. However, you can decide how you define masculinity. The society you live in may suggest that masculinity is all about athleticism, financial success, and even sexual dominance. You may also get the message that it is weak to show emotions or to talk about being afraid, hurt, or sad. This is a very limited definition of masculinity.

We hope that you choose a broader definition of masculinity. All people have feelings, and it is healthy to be open enough to experience those feelings. It is also important to allow yourself to be **vulnerable** and to be close to other people. Boys and men have a tendency to spend time with their friends doing things like playing sports and video games. They are less likely to spend time talking. To really develop closeness with someone and to give and receive support from another person, it is important to communicate. And it's surprisingly easy to get started. All you have to do is ask someone how they're doing!

Elijah's story reminds us that how we connect with people matters a great deal and how we feel about our body affects those connections. This is one of many reasons to work on developing a positive body image.

EXPERT ADVICE

Judi Craddock, author of *The Little Book of Body Confidence*, UK

"The man you are becoming has nothing to do with how your body looks. You are unique and valuable. You have more to offer the world than your appearance."

ELIJAH JACOB, 22 YEARS OLD

To those who don't know me, what seems to be the most noticeable feature of the entirety of my being is my short stature. My height has shaped how my peers perceived me, further shaping my personality. I've felt that since my height was something I could not change, I had to accept it as part of my identity. It was only relatively recently that I began to develop a personality and attitude not directed by my height. Instead of actively following the stereotypes put before me of the short, funny friend, I try to ignore them altogether. It's in this way that my body feels like a lifetime obstacle that I need to learn how to both manage and accept.

I don't pay too much attention to what I eat. Another peculiar genetic feature I inherited was a seemingly superhuman metabolism. I've averaged a weight around 100 pounds (about 45 kg), no matter what my diet has been. I still value healthy eating when I can, but my lackadaisical diet is headed by convenience rather than any dietary code.

In truth, the experiences that have most altered the way I view my body were moments of flirtation and intimacy. In all my internal dealings with my body, I had rarely considered my appearance in a positive manner. I simply bounced from a negative to neutral opinion. It was and continues to be a shock to my system when a current or prospective partner shows interest in my appearance. I'm also acutely aware that to better my mental health, I need to develop a positive body image. It's certainly a topic that pops up in therapy sessions. Hopefully, these moments of external validation will lead to a system of internal validation.

The most continually influential person in my life has been my mother. She and I have lived together on our own for the entirety of my lifetime. She is a tour de force. She grabs the attention and respect of the room with fewer words than most, even though she is several inches shorter than me. My self-doubt and hesitation are often in direct opposition to

Continued ...

her ferocity and acumen. Although we sometimes butt
heads, I do take note of how she carries herself and
approaches life.

Although I'm not exactly in a state of total body
positivity, I do feel like I have advice for younger
boys. I think it's most important for young people to
understand that as long as you're healthy, your body
is perfectly fine. We are more often judged by how
we carry ourselves, rather than by the shape of our
bodies. No one should let their body be an obstacle on
the path to discovering who they are.

REASONS FOR HOPE

Although media and celebrity culture aren't
particularly helpful in the development of positive
body images, there are reasons to hope that
change is on the way. Some **advertisers** have begun
to promote their products using body-positive
messages. Most of the obvious examples target
women, but there are also ad campaigns targeting
men that aim to promote positive body image and
mental health in general.

The Gillette ad campaign that came out in 2019 is a
great example of advertising developed to promote
healthy images of boys and men. Gillette creates
products for shaving (for example, razors, shaving
cream), but the 2019 ads didn't really focus on a
close shave or how their products smell. They began
with men looking at themselves in the mirror and
a narrator asking, "Is this the best a man can get?"
The ad featured men behaving in stereotypical sexist
ways and the narrator encouraging viewers to do
better—that these behaviors were not acceptable.
The popular saying "Boys will be boys," is refuted:
boys can do better!

This ad campaign followed the 2018 release of
guidelines by the World Federation of Advertisers for

gender portrayals and the importance of diversity in terms of both gender and culture. The Australian Association of National Advertisers also recently revised its Code of Ethics to address the importance of gender roles and the avoidance of gender stereotypes.

In addition to these advertising campaigns, there are other reasons for hope. There are body-positive and mental health **influencers** on social media. There are podcasts about body positivity and rejecting **diet culture**. And there are web pages that contain helpful resources for people looking to improve their body image. Not everyone knows about all of these resources, but hopefully that will change with time and they will inspire more and more people.

POSITIVE BODY IMAGE RESOURCES

Individual/ group	Instagram	Twitter	TikTok	Website	Description
Stevie Blaine	@bopo.boy	@bopoboy	@bopo.boy	N/A	Activist for body acceptance and the LGBTQIA+ community
Kelvin Davis	@kelvindavis	@notoriouslydapp	@notoriouslydapper	https://notoriouslydapper.com/	Author, blogger, model, and activist for body-positive gentlemen
The Every Man Project	@theeverymanproject	N/A	N/A	www.theeverymanproject.com/	Project to celebrate diversity and reject toxic masculinity
Aaron Flores	@aaronfloresrdn	N/A	N/A	http://linktr.ee/Aaronfloresrdn	Registered dietician, health at every size advocate, podcaster
Daniel Franzese	@whatsupdanny	@whatsupdanny	@whatsupdanny	https://whatsupdanny.com/	Actor, comedian, and activist for plus-size men's fashion
Nicole Groman	@thehungryclementine	@nicolegromanRD	@thehungryclementine	www.bodyovermindnutrition.com/	Registered dietician and owner of Body Over Mind Nutrition
i_weigh (Jameela Jamil)	@i_weigh	@i_weigh	@iweigh	https://iweighcommunity.com/	Actress and advocate Jameela Jamil offers information about body positivity, health, and equity
Harnaam Kaur	@harnaamkaur	@harnaamkaur	@harnaamkaurofficial	http://harnaamkaur.com/	Motivational speaker and life coach
Kavah King	@gentlemenscurb	@whosiskavahking	@kavah.king	http://gentlemenscurb.com/	Blogger and model who provides fashion inspiration and fitness tips

Name				
Zach Miko	@zachmiko	N/A	N/A	Model and body-positive influencer
Chris Mosier	@thechrismosier	N/A	www.thechrismosier.com/	First transgender athlete to make a men's US national team
Marquis Neal	N/A	@marquimode	https://linktr.ee/Marquimode	Queer model and plus-size fashion activist
Syed Sohail	@theprepguy	N/A	https://tpgstyle.com/	Photographer and fashion and lifestyle vlogger
Shana Minci Spence	@thenutritiontea	N/A	www.thenutritiontea.com	Registered dietician and eating anything nutritionist
Bruce Sturgell	@chubstr	N/A	https://chubstr.com/	Creator of blog with fashion tips and body-positive content
Jules von Hep	@julesvonhep	@julesvonhep	https://linktr.ee/julesvonhep	Social media influencer who challenges societal standards regarding male body image
Joshua Wolrich	@drjoshuawolrich	@drjoshuawolrich	https://linktr.ee/drjoshuawolrich/	Surgical doctor fighting to end weight stigma

N/A, not applicable; LGBTQIA, Lesbian, gay, bisexual, transgender, queer, intersex, and asexual.

We've previewed the above social media accounts and web pages and feel they are appropriate body-positive people for young people to be familiar with and follow. We can't anticipate what these influencers will post in the future or content that may be deemed inappropriate by some people.

BE THE CHANGE

Cultural change can be slow, but it's possible. In fact, people have not always valued the trends and fashions that we value today. A generation ago, it was not uncommon for boys and men to wear suits and ties on Sunday when they went to church or other religious services. This is much less common today, and we bet you and your friends wear casual clothes nearly always. You probably wear shorts (short pants) when the weather is warm, but this is a trend that was unimaginable 100 years ago. Across much of the 20th century, it was common for boys and men to slick their (short) hair back. Today, it is much trendier to have longer and less styled hair.

There will always be trends in terms of what our culture suggests we do to make our bodies look attractive. Some of the trends may be relatively harmless (for example, certain hairstyles), but some may be relatively dangerous (for example, supplement and steroid use). We don't have to agree with these trends or follow them. When a trend is unhealthy or even just uncomfortable, we can go our own way. If we reject certain trends, others may feel empowered to do so as well. If consumers don't buy certain products, companies will stop producing them. If we stop following certain influencers on Instagram, they may become less popular and less powerful.

We all have a role to play in creating a healthier culture. You are a "real man," no matter what hobbies you have, what clothes you wear, and what emotions you express. Be the person who takes care of yourself and others, ignores unhealthy trends, and contributes to a healthier culture for all boys and men.

As individuals, we have the power to contribute to cultural change. We can work to improve our own positive body images and we can become part of a movement where more and more boys, men, girls, and women do, as well. We can do our part to create a world where it is normal for people to appreciate their bodies—and themselves more generally—and not feel bad about who they are. What exactly would that world look like? Why don't we try to find out?

Summing Up #BeTheChange

- ☑ There are many reasons why it's important to develop a positive body image, one of which is that by exhibiting a positive body image you have the power to start to change how other people think about their bodies.

- ☑ Current attractiveness ideals and the cultural focus on our appearance can make it difficult to feel good about how we look, but it's important to work on self-compassion and self-acceptance—as well as on compassion and acceptance for others.

- ☑ Thinking about issues that are more important than how you look, and being engaged with issues that are meaningful to you, can help you develop as a well-rounded, confident person. By choosing to foster your positive body image, you set an example for those around you and help to lead society closer to understanding how important it is for all of us to be accepting and positive about who we are.

Find out more

- *The Mask You Live* In is a documentary released in 2016 that details the destructive culture of masculinity. Some of the themes of the documentary are described in this chapter and throughout this book, but the entire documentary is worth watching and can be found on YouTube: www.youtube.com/watch?v=k4yFShxUb2E.

- *Dare to Be You* (2020) by Matthew Syed is a book that will appeal to pre-teen boys interested in learning more about how to develop a positive sense of self. Publisher: Wren & Rook.

- Niobe Way is a psychologist who has done research on and written about boys' gender roles and connections with others. One of her books, *Deep Secrets: Boys' Friendships and the Crisis of Connection* (2013), addresses assumptions of masculinity and what it means to grow up male today. Publisher: Harvard University Press.

- For more scholarly articles and web pages with information about gender and body image, see the companion website for this book: www.TheBodyImageBookforBoys.com.

ASK THE EXPERTS

Here's a bit more information about the experts who provided insight, advice, and comments for this book.

Robert Atkins, PhD, RN, Acting Dean and Associate Professor of Nursing and Childhood Studies at Rutgers University; Director, New Jersey Health Initiatives of the Robert Wood Johnson Foundation, USA, https://ifh.rutgers.edu/faculty_staff/robert-l-atkins/

Zoë Bisbing, LCSW, and Leslie Bloch, LCSW-R, founders of *The Full Bloom Project* web page, podcast, and parent information about body image, www.fullbloomproject.com/about

Frank Bruni, American journalist, columnist for the *New York Times*, https://frankbruni.com/

Hayden Cedric Dawes, LCSW, LCAS, www.hcdawes.com/about

Judi Craddock, body image coach, author of *The Little Book of Body Confidence*, https://heartyourbody.co.uk/

Adam Fare, eating disorders activist, www.youtube.com/watch?v=hiOzAkO Z80

Georgie Fear, RD, CSSD, author of *Give Yourself MORE*, http://georgiefear.com/

Rebekah Fenton, MD, Adolescent Medicine Fellow at Lurie Children's Hospital/Northwestern University Feinberg School of Medicine, USA, www.pediatrics.northwestern.edu/education/fellows/adolescent/fellows.html

Ed Frauenheim, Former Senior Director of Content at Great Place to Work, co-author of *Reinventing Masculinity: The Liberating Power of Compassion and Connection*, www.linkedin.com/in/ed-frauenheim-685294/

Matthew Fuller-Tyszkiewicz, PhD, Professor at Deakin University, Centre for Social and Early Emotional Development, Australia, www.deakin.edu.au/about-deakin/people/matthew-fuller-tyszkiewicz

Scott Griffiths, PhD, Professor at University of Melbourne, Melbourne School of Psychological Sciences, Australia, https://unimelb.academia.edu/ScottGriffiths

Oona Hanson, MA, MA, parent coach, health advocate, family mentor with Equip eating disorders treatment, www.oonahanson.com/

Jeffrey Hunger, PhD, Assistant Professor, Department of Psychology, Miami University, USA, http://jeffreyhunger.com/index.html

Yaffi Lvova, RDN, founder of *Baby Bloom Nutrition, Toddler Test Kitchen and Nap Time Nutrition*, https://babybloomnutrition.com/

Marita McCabe, PhD, Professor, Health and Aging Research Group, Swinburn University, Australia, www.uqac.ca/abeh/index.php/marita-mccabe/

Cody Miller, Olympic gold and bronze medalist in swimming and six-time World Championship medalist, www.teamusa.org/usa-swimming/athletes/Cody-Miller

Chris Mosier, duathlete, triathlete, and first transgender athlete to make it on to the US National Team in the gender in which they identify, www.thechrismosier.com/about-1

Stuart Murray, PhD, Associate Professor, Department of Psychiatry and Behavioral Sciences, University of Southern California, USA, Director of the Eating Disorders Program and Director of the Translational Research in Eating Disorders Laboratory, https://keck.usc.edu/faculty-search/stuart-murray/

Jason Nagata, MD, MSc, Assistant Professor, Division of Adolescent & Young Adult Medicine, University of California, San Francisco, USA, https://pediatrics.ucsf.edu/faculty/jason-nagata

Cara Natterson, MD, author of *Guy Stuff, Decoding Boys, and The Care and Keeping of You*, as well as other books, www.worryproofmd.com/

Gemma Sharp, PhD, Senior Research Fellow and clinical psychologist, leader of the Body Image Research Group at Monash University, Australia, https://research.monash.edu/en/persons/gemma-sharp

Jaclyn Siegel, PhD, postdoctoral researcher and project director, Pride Body Project, San Diego State University, USA, www.jaclynasiegel.com/

Virginia Sole-Smith, journalist and author of *The Eating Instinct*, co-host of *Comfort Food Podcast*, https://virginiasolesmith.com/

Tracy Tylka, PhD, Professor of Psychology, Ohio State University, USA; editor of *Body Image: An International Journal of Research*, https://psychology.osu.edu/people/tylka.2

Timothy Wenger, founder of The Man Effect, www.themaneffect.com

Zali Yager, PhD, Associate Professor, Victoria University, Australia, Executive director of The Body Confidence Collective, www.zaliyager.com

ACKNOWLEDGMENTS

From Charlotte

I feel so fortunate to have had an opportunity to work on this book for boys and am incredibly grateful to everyone who helped to make this book possible. First, I want to thank my co-authors, Dan (my husband and the best psychologist and writer I know) and Doug (whose youthful enthusiasm we needed), for agreeing to go on this journey with me. I wouldn't dream of embarking on writing a prescriptive resource for boys without thoughtful men in my corner. I appreciate their willingness to answer all of the uncomfortable questions I threw at them about growing up male.

I am grateful to many people at Cambridge University Press for believing in my vision, being generous with resources to bring this project to fruition, and being so incredibly supportive. Sarah Marsh believed in this project long before I even began it and I'm certain that without her, *Being You* would not exist today. Knowing that we were writing for her boys and others like them was an inspiration. Kim Ingram and Saskia Pronk have helped keep us organized throughout the long process of putting a book together. Lori Handelman is an amazing editor and has helped me to become a better writer. Dan Bramall, our amazing illustrator, helped to bring this book to life and also provided a fabulous cover design. I know that many boys will read this book only because he has made it look fun, youthful, and dynamic. Zoe Naylor also brought her fantastic artistic vision for the entire book in creating the design and layout of the pages.

No one would know about these books without the many amazing people involved in marketing who have lined up interviews, sent books to the right people, and convinced thousands to look at my books. Danny Bean, has been offering incredible support since the early days of our work on *The Body Image Book for Girls* and I'm grateful that Maddy Boles is now on our team as well. Chris Burrows has helped us to spread the word in the UK, while Megan Beatie led efforts stateside. I am also grateful to Kim Dower and Susie Stangland for helping me hone my (social) media skills.

I am indebted to my colleagues and friends who have indulged my never-ending desire to discuss the issues we've written about in this book, especially Kristin August, Laurie Bernstein Jamie Dunaev, Meghan Gillen, Oona Hanson, Jennifer Rappaport, Amy Sepinwall, and Lorie Sousa. Thank you to the many people including researchers, clinicians, health advocates, and journalists who provided expert quotes for this book. I appreciate all of the work they do to spread positive body image and their willingness to contribute their voices to this book.

I am thankful for my graduate and undergraduate students and research assistants who have been an invaluable source of help and encouragement, including Stacey Alston, Nana Amponsah, Jordan Bergman, Sofia Bonsignore, William Fitzgerald, Erika Frick, Trista Harig, Nicole Holmes, Samantha Kehner, Maxine Koza, Steysi Lara, Jo Abby Lods, Dua Malik, Shannon McGlinn, Hemali Patel, Mendy-Keyla Tossou, Kennedy Tran, and Eric Zavadsky. I am also grateful to John Crowell, who was instrumental when we initiated this project and began to interview boys.

Of course, this book is for and about boys, and I am grateful to all of the boys and men who allowed us to interview them and who participated in focus groups to discuss book content, including Nathan Allred, Cole Beck-Campell, Dylan Bidoli, Carl Borgstrom, Joel Caputo, Steve Chile, Callum Coughlin, Jason Danielewicz, Confesor Diaz, Harris Faisal, Adam Fare, Jack Gainey, Brody Gallagher, James Gelleher, Carter Grunseich, Aaden Guarino, Jasper Hals, Ricky Harig, Ronny Healey, Howard Jones, Manush Kathrotia, Mehul Khedekar, Cameron Kienow, Kyle King, Irving Lopez, Adrian Lynch, Ryan Lynch, Matt McConnell, Louis Parker, Parth Patel, Tyler Rudolph, Mane Sevilla, Gavin Schmidt, Ethan Shaw Stolar, and Wyatt Stevens.

Finally, I am grateful to my family, including my mom and the kids I feel so incredibly privileged to watch grow up, Charlie and Grace.

From Dan

Thanks to my co-authors for inviting me to join them in writing a book that we hope will help boys grow into healthy adulthood. Like Doug, I've learned a lot from Charlotte about how to make science accessible to young audiences. If this book is successful, it's because Charlotte has developed the formula for writing effectively about important issues for tweens and teens.

My contributions to the book are based in part on my decades of research and teaching as a developmental psychologist. My work is also informed by 40 years of living with children and teenagers who have met life's challenges with courage and optimism. My eternal gratitude goes to Matthew, Sarah, Norman, John, Tyquane, Hasan, Abdoulaye, Charlie, and Grace for sharing your lives and illuminating mine.

From Doug

First, I want to thank Charlotte and Dan for allowing me to work on a project like this with them. It's such an honor to have the opportunity to work with such accomplished and esteemed individuals.

I want to thank Kristin August for helping get me involved in the project and being an incredible mentor to me at each stage of my career. I'd also like to thank Robrecht van der Wel and Sean Duffy for their support.

I'm grateful to my partner, Alanna G. Durkin, for supporting me, and reminding me that the voice in my head that says "I can't do it" is wrong.

I want to acknowledge my father, Jim Zacher, for directly and indirectly shaping me into the person I am today.

Finally, I want to thank my mother, Debbi Nanni. She is always in my corner, is an inspiration to me, and is one of the reasons I know I am enough being exactly who I am.

GLOSSARY

Acceptance (see self-acceptance): Approving of something without wanting to change anything about it.

Acne (pimples, spots, breakout): A skin condition where pores become clogged with oil, bacteria, and dead skin cells, resulting in an inflamed eruption of the skin.

Active: Involving physical movement or action.

Activists (activism): People who participate, get involved in, campaign for, or bring awareness to a certain situation and act on it to make a change.

Adaptive appearance investment: Regularly engaging in appearance-related self-care, such as grooming behaviors that protect an individual's sense of style and personality. Usually includes enhancing one's natural features via non-harmful methods.

Adolescence: The stage of physical and mental development that occurs between childhood and adulthood; this stage is often marked by the onset of puberty.

Advertising (advertiser, advertisement): A form of communication that markets or promotes a message in order to sell something.

American Academy of Pediatrics (AAP): A large organization of doctors in the USA that focuses on kids' health.

American Psychological Association: The largest professional organization for psychologists in the USA; their main goal is to further grow and develop the field of psychology.

American Society of Plastic Surgeons: A large organization of plastic surgeons in the USA.

Analyze: To closely study or research something.

Anorexia nervosa: A type of eating disorder usually characterized by a fear of gaining weight; those with anorexia try to become or remain underweight by depriving themselves of food or by exercising excessively. People do not need to be underweight to be anorexic.

Anti-anxiety medication: Medication that alters the chemicals in a person's brain and can make them feel calmer and happier.

Antidepressant medication: Medication that alters the chemicals in a person's brain to alleviate symptoms of depression.

Anxiety disorder: Constant feelings of worry, anxiety, or fear that interferes with a person's daily life.

Artificial sweetener: A food additive that provides a sweet taste in place of actual sugar, while also providing few to no calories.

Athletic: Relating to sports; muscular, strong in shape.

Beauty sick(ness): Spending energy worrying about appearance at the cost of focusing on things like education, careers, family, and relationships.

Behaviors (behavioral habits): The way in which a person acts, or does something; a regular way of doing something, a routine.

Benzoyl peroxide: A medicine used to treat acne and other skin conditions.

Binge(ing): A brief period of time in which a person will indulge excessively on a substance, usually consuming a lot of food or alcohol quickly.

Binge eating disorder (BED): An eating disorder that involves binging (at least once a week for at least 3 months) without purging. Binges are described as excessive in terms of how much is eaten and they're experienced as uncontrollable.

Blogger: A person who writes for a blog, which is usually an online publication of some sort.

Blood cholesterol (see cholesterol): When the body has too much cholesterol and it gets stuck in the blood vessels, it can contribute to heart disease.

Body dysmorphic disorder (BDD): A body image disorder. People with BDD focus on their body's flaws and are preoccupied with trying to fix flaws that are usually not noticeable to other people.

Body image: How you think or feel about your body; how you view yourself on a day-to-day basis.

Body neutrality: When a person doesn't dislike their body, but they don't put pressure on themselves to love their body all the time, either.

Body odor (BO): The different scents the human body gives off; can become unpleasant (or stinky) when sweat mixes with bacteria that are found naturally on the skin.

#BoPo: A hashtag for body-positive posts on social media.

Botox (botulinum toxin): A drug made from the toxins of Clostridium botulinum bacteria. This toxin is what causes botulism, but it can also have many medical and cosmetic uses such as improving the appearance of wrinkles.

British Psychological Society: An organization that represents psychologists in the UK and strives to promote excellence and ethical practices in education, research, and the provision of psychological services.

Bulimia nervosa: An eating disorder that typically involves binging and then purging food.

Breakout: see acne.

Bully (tease): To tease or mess with someone; to aim to make a person feel inferior.

Bulking: Excessively eating, often specific types of food, while lifting heavy weights to gain muscle.

Calorie(s): A unit of measurement to assess the amount of energy in a certain food; a unit of measurement used to describe the energy potential of a substance.

Cancer: A disease that is caused by an uncontrolled growth of abnormal cells in a part of the body.

Carb loading: Often used by athletes when they have a big race or game; eating meals with a lot of carbohydrates in them, like bread and pasta, to give the body energy quickly.

Carbohydrates (carbs): An organic compound that's an easy source of energy; carbs may help fuel athletic performance.

Centered: emotionally calm and comfortable with oneself.

Centers for Disease Control and Prevention (CDC): A national public health agency and institution in the USA.

Cheat meal: A meal that is different from the diet plan one is trying to follow.

Chocoholic: How a person who feels as though they're "addicted" to chocolate may describe themselves.

Cholesterol: Fatty substance that's carried around the body in the blood. There is "good" (high density) and "bad" (low density) cholesterol.

Circumcised (circumcision): The removal of the skin, called the foreskin, that covers the top of the penis. Usually, if this is removed, it is done in the hospital on the first day or so following a boy's birth, or during a religious ceremony when a boy is a baby.

Commitment strategy: A strategy developed to help one stick to a goal; for example, telling people about your goals and asking for help in achieving them.

Compassion(ate) (see self-compassion): To show caring, understanding, and kindness to a person and/or the issues a person is dealing with.

Compulsive exercise: When exercising feels like an obligation to a person, not something enjoyed; exercise that a person feels is necessary, maybe more than once per day.

Confidence: Feeling certain about oneself and one's abilities.

Consent(ed): When a person has specifically stated that they are comfortable and agree with what is going to happen.

Cosmetics: Relating to a person's appearance, or products for a person's appearance (for example, make-up).

Covering: Hiding a part of yourself so that you can fit in.

Cutting: Describes efforts to gain noticeable muscle by restricting foods eaten to lose weight following weightlifting for an excessive amount of time.

Cyberbullying (see bullying): Bullying or teasing that takes place online.

Dairy: Any and all products that contain milk (cheese, yogurt, ice cream, butter, etc.).

Density: Thickness or heaviness.

Depressed (depression, depressing): A feeling a person gets where they simply cannot become happy; they remain in a sad 'funk' or mood. Depression is also a mental health disorder when it's a lasting negative mood and/or outlook on life.

Dermatologist: A doctor who specializes in skin care.

Despair: To feel hopeless, distressed.

Dextrose: A type of sugar.

Diabetes: A condition where a person's body doesn't make any or makes too little of a certain hormone (insulin) that regulates sugar levels in the body (type 1 diabetes), or where the person's body can't process a certain kind of sugar (type 2 diabetes).

Diet: How or what a person eats. A specific plan of foods to be eaten either to lose weight or for medical reasons.

Diet culture: Includes the fads and messaging that suggest the importance of weight loss and constant self-improvement.

Dietician (see nutritionist): An expert who studies food and nutrition. Dieticians teach people what to eat in order to have a healthy lifestyle and/or manage health

problems related to illness and disease. Formal schooling, training, and certification are required to be considered a dietician.

Dysphoria: A feeling of unhappiness, uneasiness, or dissatisfaction with life.

Eating disorders: Category of conditions/illnesses that involve troublesome eating habits that can lead to serious problems and even death.

Ejaculation: Release of semen (usually containing sperm) from the penis after an orgasm.

Embarrassed (embarrassment): A feeling that a person gets when unwanted attention is focused on him, similar to shame, awkwardness, and self-consciousness.

Embodiment: The sense of "being in touch with" or "happily living in" your body.

Empower (empowering): To encourage, support or make a person feel more confident in themselves and their abilities.

Energy: The strength and activity you're able to experience derived from the amount of calories consumed.

Enhance (enhancements): To increase or upgrade something; improvements.

Erection: Occurs when blood flows to the penis causing the soft tissue of the penis to grow firm. It may occur when a person touches their own penis, someone else touches it, a person feels excited or nervous, or for no reason at all.

Evaluate: To judge or analyze something.

Evidence-based information: Information that comes from research that uses a scientific method; information based on scientific evidence.

Exercise: A particular type of physical activity that's usually planned and purposeful.

Exertion: Physical or mental effort; extra work or strain involved in doing a task.

Fad: Something (like a diet, fashion or make-up trend) that becomes widely popular, but the hype goes away quickly; a trend or short-lived popularity.

Fast(ing): Not eating or drinking all or some kinds of foods and drinks, sometimes for a religious observance or for weight loss.

Fast food: Inexpensive yet filling food that is prepared quickly and easily.

Fats: A type of nutrient that the body uses for fuel and to store energy.

Fiber: Food that isn't digested or absorbed by the body.

Filter: A technique that changes the look of an image, usually to refine and improve certain aspects of the image.

Fitness: Relating to exercise and being physically activity; the condition of how healthy or strong someone is.

Fitspiration ("fitspo"): Words, images, and videos that are intended to serve as motivation or inspiration to improve health and fitness.

Flexitarian: People who are "sometimes vegetarians" who mostly eat a vegetarian diet.

FOMO: Stands for the "fear of missing out."

Food addiction: A food habit that a person may experience, but that doesn't involve a chemical dependency (alcohol and drug addictions typically involve a chemical dependency). Food addiction isn't considered an eating disorder by psychologists.

Food and Drug Administration (FDA): The US national federal agency that's responsible for the safety of food, medical drugs, and cosmetic products that humans and pets consume and/or use. The FDA doesn't monitor or control products including vitamins and supplements.

Food restriction: To cut out a significant portion of food (or food groups), usually for weight loss, or for a health concern (such as diabetes).

Functionality: The ability to perform and serve a specific purpose (legs serve the purpose or function of walking, running, etc.).

Genitals: Male and female reproductive body parts (for men, the penis; for women, the vagina).

Groom(ing): To clean up or make neat.

Growth spurt: A period of time during puberty in which a boy or girl grows several inches.

Hangry: Being so hungry that a person becomes angry or irritable in some cases (angry + hungry = hangry).

Harassment (see sexual harassment): Any type of behavior that can be seen as offensive, inappropriate, and hurtful to another person.

Health at Every Size Movement (HAES): An anti-diet, body positivity, and diversity acceptance movement that suggests it is important for people to focus on healthy habits, no matter their size.

Healthy: Physical, mental, and emotional wellness; free from illness or disease.

Healthy media diet: A limited use of media or certain types of media. It often refers to parents putting restrictions on their children's screen time, especially to ensure that it doesn't interfere with their children's sleep.

Heart disease: A condition where a passageway into the heart can be blocked, or something is wrong with the heart's muscles.

High-fructose corn syrup: A sweetener frequently used in commercially produced foods and drinks that is made from cornstarch as a cheaper alternative to sucrose (other sugar products).

High-intensity interval training (HIIT): Exercise routines or workouts that involve alternating between nearly all-out exertion (for example, running absolutely as fast as you can) and lower exertion (for example, jogging) for intervals of a minute each (or some other set times).

Highlight reel: A slang term used to describe a quick summary of the most relevant high points of someone's experiences or life.

Hormones: Chemicals the body produces that alter and control bodily functions. For example, there are hormones that alter feelings of hunger, sleepiness, and even happiness.

Hygiene: Cleanliness; practicing cleanliness for health and proper body care.

Influencer (social media influencer): A popular and influential social media user; a person who is used to promote certain items to persuade others to buy products.

Insecure (insecurities): To feel unconfident, doubtful, or unsure of oneself.

Instincts: A natural tendency, something a person may do without realizing it.

Intermittent fasting: To limit food eaten overall by reducing what's eaten during certain periods of time in a day or week. For example, a person may eat regularly for 5 days a week and then eat relatively little for a couple of days a week, or a person may eat within a select window of time each day.

Internalize (internalizing): To take information that's outside of you and make it your own; to believe a thought, attitude, or behavior of others and make it yours—usually without realizing it.

International Society for Aesthetic Plastic Surgery: An international group of surgeons with expertise in plastic and cosmetic surgery. The group promotes the sharing of information among medical professionals and the public.

Intuitive eating: The process of listening to the body's signals of hungry and fullness and eating what's appealing, satisfying, and healthy.

Invest(ing) (investment): To put time, money, or effort into something in order to gain something new in return.

Ironic processing: A term that describes trying to clear your mind of something, which then has the opposite effect. For example, if you tell someone to not think about chocolate, they may end up thinking about it more than they would have if you hadn't told them that.

Juice concentrate: Juice from fruit that is processed or filtered to remove water.

Ketogenic diet: A high-fat and low-carbohydrate (carb) diet. This sort of diet typically allows eating foods including vegetables that grow above ground, eggs, seafood, unprocessed meats, high-fat dairy products, and berries.

Kilocalorie (kcal) (see calorie): A measurement used to determine the energy value of food.

Kilogram (kg): A unit of measurement. One kilogram is equal to 2.2 pounds and 0.16 stone.

Lifestyle: The way in which a person or group of people live; this can include career, culture, social class, and interests. For example, the lifestyle of a celebrity and a school teacher may be very different.

Literate (literacy): The knowledge and understanding of a particular topic, subject, or field of study.

Macrobiotic eaters: Vegans who only eat unprocessed foods and sometimes fish; they also avoid sugar and refined oils.

Majority: An amount that makes up the greater part of the whole.

Manipulate: To control or influence something, especially in order to deceive or mislead someone.

Masturbation: When a person rubs their genitals to feel good. Sometimes referred to as "whacking off," "jerking off," or "wanking."

Mayo Clinic: A world-famous, non-profit medical academic and research hospital, originally in Minnesota but with other locations as well, that also has an online database containing information about certain diseases and illnesses.

Media: Any form of mass communication, which includes broadcasting (such as cable television, streaming), the internet (such as social media), and publications like newspapers (such as *The New York Times*).

Media literate (media literacy): Knowledge and understanding of the media, and how and why it functions the way it does; how to interpret information available in media.

Meditation: A variety of different techniques aimed to train the mind to be calm.

Meme: A funny, popular image or video that's widely spread and shared online—especially on social media.

Mental health: Relating to a person's mental and emotional health and well-being.

Metabolism: The chemical processes that take place within the body that are essential to keep us alive.

Micronutrients: Vitamins and minerals that are needed to keep the body healthy; usually found in food.

Mindful(ness): A practice of being aware of oneself and one's thoughts, feelings, physical body and physical surroundings.

Mindless eating: To eat something without enjoying the process of eating; sometimes eating without even being hungry, out of boredom.

Minerals: Solid substances that occur in nature.

Misbeliefs: A misconception; a wrong belief or misunderstanding, based on an error in thinking or judgment.

Moderation: To have something within limits, or a balance; not having too much or too little of something.

Motivate (motivation): To encourage someone to do something; to feel inspired or eager to do something.

Muscle dysmorphia: Sometimes referred to as the "male eating disorder" or

"bigorexia." A subtype of body dysmorphic disorder, and more of a body image disorder than an eating disorder.

Muscular: Relating to muscles; strong or well-developed muscles.

My Plate: The US government's description of what to eat if we're trying to be healthy; it includes a focus on fruits and vegetables as approximately half of all foods eaten.

Myths: Stories or explanations that are sometimes passed around by communities to explain things that are not well understood.

National Eating Disorder Association: An American non-profit organization focused on eating-disorder prevention and treatment, as well as education regarding eating disorders, weight, and body image.

National Institute on Drug Abuse: A US government agency that aims to advance research and treatment concerning addiction.

Natural supplements: A type of dietary supplement that contains one or more plant-based products. Supplements can affect health but are not regulated by the Food and Drug Administration (FDA) in the USA and may contain toxic ingredients. Supplements are regulated in some other countries, including the UK.

Nocturnal emission: Also known as a "wet dream." Occurs when a boy experiences an erection and then ejaculates in his sleep (often while dreaming).

Non-profit organization: An organization that has a goal to provide aid, services, and contribute to an important cause. These organizations don't aim to make money, and any money that they obtain through donations or fundraising is used to further their organization's goals.

Nourish(ment): To provide with food or other substances necessary for health and development.

Nutrition: Pertaining to the essential components of food that are needed to support health.

Nutritional value: Related to the amount of nutrients in a particular food.

Nutritionist: A professional who studies food and nutrition. They teach people what to eat in order to have a healthy lifestyle and/or manage health problems related to illness and disease. Unlike a dietician, legal certification is not required to be considered a nutritionist.

Nutritious: Describes types of foods that are good for the body and likely to improve health.

Objectify (objectified, objectification): To treat someone like they are an object.

Obsessive-compulsive disorder (OCD): An anxiety disorder that typically includes being a perfectionist, orderly, and neat, and experiencing intense anxiety when this is not possible.

Orthorexia: An overconcern with healthy eating that can be psychologically damaging. Although it is not a clinical diagnosis, orthorexia is often described as an eating disorder.

Other specified feeding or eating disorder: This is a long way of saying someone has an "other eating disorder" that can disrupt their life, and can lead to drastic weight gain or weight loss. A clinical eating-disorder diagnosis that applies to individuals who aren't considered to have anorexia nervosa, bulimia nervosa, or binge eating disorder.

Overweight: Above what's considered "normal weight" for a person's height by the medical community.

Ovo-lacto vegetarians: Vegetarians who do eat eggs and drink milk, also known as lacto-ovo vegetarians.

Paleo (diet): Sometimes referred to as the caveman diet; a type of diet that's based on foods similar to what might have been eaten during the Paleolithic era (approximately 2.5 million to 10,000 years ago). A paleo diet typically includes fruits, vegetables, lean meats, fish, nuts, and seeds.

Pediatrician: A doctor who deals with the health and wellness of children, usually ages 17 and below.

Penis: A male's genitals/sex organ.

Personality: The sum of traits that makes up a person's character; a person's non-physical identity.

Pescatarian(ism): A person who doesn't eat meat but eats fish; a type of vegetarianism.

Photoshop: A type of software used to alter photographs; to digitally change an image using a program such as Adobe Photoshop.

Physical activity: Any kind of movement of the body.

Physical dependency: When the body depends on a substance to continue to function, such as a drug that creates a dependency, and discontinuing use of it would result in serious and unpleasant withdrawal symptoms.

Pimples: see acne.

Pornography: Printed or digital imagery or text containing sexually explicit content.

Portray (portrayal): To represent or show something/someone in a specific way.

Positive: Confident, optimistic, happy, or good.

Positive body image: Favorable opinions about the body, body acceptance, respect for the body, taking care of the body, and rejecting unrealistic standards of physical beauty.

Potassium: A type of mineral found in food that's good for the body; it helps with normal muscle growth and helps maintain water in the body.

Preservative: Something put into food to make it last longer and not spoil as quickly as a natural or unpreserved food.

Processed food: Food that's altered before people eat it. Processed foods usually have a lot of sugar, salt, and possibly fats added to them to improve their taste.

Protective filtering: The process of filtering out influences in a person's life that negatively affects his or her body image.

Protein: An important nutrient needed to help and protect various parts of the body including bones, muscles, cartilage, and skin.

Psychological disorders: A wide range of mental health conditions that affect mood, thinking, and behavior. Psychological disorders include eating disorders, depression, and anxiety.

Psychologist: A scientist who studies the human mind, including how people think, feel, and behave. Some psychologists provide therapy to help people talk through their problems or mental health disorders.

Puberty: The physical and hormonal changes that lead a child's body to grow into an adult body; this process is marked by the development of secondary sex characteristics (pubic hair, and facial hair) and the ability to sexually reproduce.

Pubic hair: Body hair that appears on the genitals or in the genital regions during puberty.

Purging: Any means of ridding the body of food eaten; it can include taking medication that leads one to vomit or get diarrhea or exercising extensively.

Rhabdomyolysis: The breakdown or "death" of muscle fibers, which releases myoglobin (a protein) into the bloodstream and can result in a serious health problem.

Realistic (see unrealistic): To be considered truthful, attainable or reasonable.

Regimen: A kind of plan that may involve a medical treatment, diet, or a general lifestyle change.

Researcher (scientist): A person who has experience in, is considered an expert in, and studies a specific topic related to science.

Respect: To hold in high esteem or deep admiration.

Revealing: Showing more of something than usual; for example, revealing clothes show more of a person's body or a part of the body than usual.

Salicylic acid: An anti-inflammatory medication that treats acne and other skin conditions.

Salt: Also known as sodium chloride; it's used to preserve foods and make foods taste better.

Saturated fats: A type of fat; a less healthy fat than unsaturated fats; found in most

dairy and meat products.

Savoring: Eating or drinking and enjoying the experience completely.

Science (scientific evidence): The study of the world by observations and experiments, usually by trained professionals (scientists).

Screen time: The amount of time spent using an electronic device, such as a phone, tablet, computer, or television.

Scrotum: Part of the male reproductive system; a sac of skin that holds the testicles.

Self-acceptance: The attitude of being comfortable with yourself, the good and the bad, without wanting to change for others' approval.

Self-care: Taking care of yourself physically, emotionally, and mentally, especially during stressful times.

Self-compassion: To be understanding, patient, and kind to yourself, especially when feeling dissatisfied with your appearance, thoughts, or behaviors.

Self-conscious (see insecure): To feel uncomfortable about yourself; nervous, tense, or shy.

Self-presentation (presentation): How people present themselves to others to create a certain narrative about themselves, and how they want other people to view them.

Semen: Reproductive fluid that comes from the penis; it contains sperm and other fluid.

Semenarche: The development period of sperm, which begins during puberty.

Sexting: The act of sending sexually suggestive/explicit photos or text messages to another person.

Shave: Removing hair from the body with a razor.

Shredded/shredding: When a person has big muscles and muscle definition. A person works toward muscle definition or getting ripped.

Social circle: A group of people socially connected in one form or another. For example, a person may be a part of a small group of friends within a big group of friends; both would be considered social circles.

Social comparison: When a person compares themselves with other people to determine their worth in some feature, or as a way to see how they measure up against another.

Social media: A group of social websites and electronic applications (apps) that allow people to socialize, create, and share content with others within a digital network.

Society: A large group of people living together within a community.

Sociologist: A scientist who studies social issues, social institutions, and society in general.

Soda: A carbonated drink that is typically regarded as bad for one's health. It tends to contain no nutrients and may contain a lot of sugar or sugar substitutes.

Software: The digital programs and operations within an electronic device (such as a cell phone, computer, or game console).

Spermarche: The first ejaculation of sperm, which usually occurs among boys during puberty while they are sleeping.

Spontaneous erections: Erections that occur for what seem to be no reason at all. Spontaneous erections are common during adolescence and are a normal occurrence.

Spots: see acne.

St. John's Wort: A supplement that is often described as helpful to treating depression, but can actually interfere with other medications and may lead to unwanted side effects.

Steroids: Pills or injections that may enhance speed or muscle mass, but their use can be really harmful to health. They are illegal and their use is not allowed among professional athletes.

Stereotypes: A common but overly simple idea about a type of person (for example all boys) or thing.

Stigmatize: Judging someone as lesser because they have a particular quality or due to a circumstance; to regard someone with disapproval due to a feature such as their body size, gender, race, or religion.

Stress: A state of physical, mental, or emotional strain usually caused by struggling to deal with a difficult situation.

Stressed (see stress): To be in a state of stress.

Stretch marks: Marks on the body that typically develop due to quick gains or losses in weight including rapid growth during puberty; most men and women have some stretch marks.

Stylist: A person who dresses up or does someone's make-up and hair in a stylish, professional manner.

Substance use disorders: An addiction to a substance. Individuals with an addiction are unable to control use of an illegal or legal drug or medication.

Suicide: Self-harm that is intended to result in death.

Sugar: Sweet-tasting nutrient that's often desired and added to a lot of food to improve its taste.

Superficial: Shallow or surface level, not deep or meaningful.

Tax: A required, added cost to a product, such as a clothing purchase.

Tease: see bully.

Technique: A specific, often skillful way of doing something.

Testicles: Also known as "balls." Round organs that are enclosed in the scrotum and are located behind the penis. This is where sperm are produced.

Testosterone: Hormone produced in the testes of men that's responsible for the development and maintenance of traits such as facial hair, deep voice, and muscle growth.

Toiletries: Products used to clean the body (hygiene products) or otherwise care for the body, such as soap, toothpaste, and lotion.

Top surgery: A surgical procedure for transgender men to remove breast tissue and make the chest appear more masculine.

Toxic masculinity: A term used to describe a strict following of male gender roles such as being independent and behaving in ways that express dominance toward others, especially women.

Underweight: Below normal weight for a person's height and age according to the medical community.

Unhealthy: Something that can be harmful to one's health.

Unrealistic: Unreasonable; very difficult or impossible to do or obtain.

Unsaturated fat: a type of fat often referred to as "healthy fat" that can be found in foods such as avocados, nuts, and olive oil.

Vegan(ism): Specific diet that doesn't include any meat or dairy products.

Vegetarian(ism): Specific diet that doesn't include meat and products made with meat (for example chicken, pork, fish, beef).

Vitamins: Important elements found in foods that contribute to health and are sometimes taken in pill form.

Vulnerable: To feel unsafe, unprotected, or overly exposed.

Water retention: When fluid builds up inside the body. A common symptom is swelling in the hands and feet. Sometimes called fluid retention or edema.

Weight stigma (weight bias/weight-based discrimination): When a person is viewed unfavorably or mistreated because he or she is overweight. For example, a person may be assumed to be lazy or addicted to junk food, just because he has a larger body.

Well-being: A person's state of comfort and health.

Withdrawal: Unpleasant and potentially dangerous physical and mental symptoms that occur when stopping or reducing intake of a drug once a dependency has developed for it.

World Health Organization (WHO): An organization focused on international public health.

INDEX